Praise for

GOOD AND BEAUTIFUL AND KIND

"*Good and Beautiful and Kind* is a peaceful, gracious, and wise formulation of what it looks like to follow Jesus in a world ripping apart by a lack of love, by systemic powers, and by our own woundedness. One will not find a cajoling gospel here but a deeply gracious and good gospel that not only can heal us personally but can repair our fractured society. Give yourself a retreat to spend time with this beautiful book."

—Rev. Canon Dr. Scot McKnight,
professor of New Testament at Northern Seminary

"We desperately need resources to heal the brokenness, deception, and deformation that has crept into the church. In this beautiful book, Rich Villodas lays out a vision, theology, framework, and life-giving practices to help us restore our integrity and become more like the disciples Jesus had in mind. I am deeply grateful for his pastoral, analytical, and compelling vision."

—Jon Tyson, author of *Beautiful Resistance*
and pastor of Church of the City New York

"This book is a gift to us all! Every chapter is incredible. So timely and important. Grace-filled, hope-filled, practical, and thought-provoking. Rich not only identifies the fractures in our world and wounds in our souls, but he also provides a pathway to wholeness. *Good and Beautiful and Kind* is written from the heart of a true pastor who longs for people to know 'we were made in love and for love by a good, beautiful, and kind God.' In a broken and disillusioned world, these pages are full of hope and healing. You will discover that the ancient way of Jesus is actually the path to the future."

—CHRISTINE CAINE, founder of A21 and Propel Women

"Reconciliation and justice require new frameworks and practices to reach the next generation. In this book, Rich Villodas has given us a path toward goodness, beauty, and kindness when we are rooted in the way of Jesus. This is a must-read for everyone longing for wholeness and healing."

—LATASHA MORRISON, founder and CEO of Be the Bridge, and the *New York Times* bestselling author of *Be the Bridge: Pursuing God's Heart for Racial Reconciliation,* ECPA 2021 Christian Book of the Year

"With his characteristic blend of theological insight and keen analysis of the human condition, Rich Villodas helps us look closely at the forces that are tearing us and our world apart. He moves us tenderly and pastorally toward practices that can help us find healing—personally, relationally, and socially. If the church has any hope of recovering its radiance, it will be the result of the kind of deep work Rich leads us to embrace here. This is a stunning book with significant power to reshape our world . . . if we let it."

—GLENN PACKIAM, pastor and author of *The Resilient Pastor* and *Blessed Broken Given*

"It's not a secret that we are living in difficult and fractured times. Not only do we know this; we *feel* this. Such times can be reasons for not just helplessness but more dangerously, *hopelessness.* Thankfully, there are servant leaders like Pastor Rich Villodas who don't pretend to have all the answers and yet are not afraid to invite us to walk 'a better way.' In his latest book, Villodas offers us an honest, reflective, and faithful compass to guide us to more of a good, beautiful, and kind life. How do I know a book is good? When my soul feels heard, encouraged, and challenged to keep pursuing and embodying the kingdom of God. Such is this book!"

—REV. EUGENE CHO, president and CEO of Bread for the World, and author of *Thou Shalt Not Be a Jerk: A Christian's Guide to Engaging Politics*

"Many would confess that we are living in a fractured and anxious age. Still, few people have moved us from diagnosis to healing. In *Good and Beautiful and Kind,* Rich charts, with masterful insight and pastoral clarity, both the root causes of the dis-ease of our time and the spiritual antidotes that can lead to wholeness. For those of us praying, longing, and waiting for wholeness, this is an answered prayer. What a gift!"

—REV. DR. GABRIEL SALGUERO, pastor of the Gathering Place and president of the National Latino Evangelical Coalition

"So much in the world right now seems so wrong. What can keep us going another day? *Good and Beautiful and Kind* by Rich Villodas restores a sense of joy and sweetness on the journey of discipleship. This book is for all those who need a reminder that even when times seem dim, there is a path that leads to brightness and abundant life."

—JEMAR TISBY, PHD, author of *The Color of Compromise* and *How to Fight Racism*

GOOD
AND
BEAUTIFUL
AND
KIND

BECOMING WHOLE IN A
FRACTURED WORLD

RICH VILLODAS

WATERBROOK

2023 WaterBrook Trade Paperback Edition

Copyright © 2022 by Richard A. Villodas, Jr.

A Guide for Reflection and Discussion copyright © 2023 by Richard A. Villodas, Jr.

Foreword by Ann Voskamp copyright © 2022
by Penguin Random House LLC

All rights reserved.

Published in the United States by WaterBrook,
an imprint of Random House, a division of
Penguin Random House LLC.

WATERBROOK and colophon are registered trademarks
of Penguin Random House LLC.

Originally published in hardcover and in slightly different form by WaterBrook, an imprint of Random House, a division of Penguin Random House LLC, in 2022.

Grateful acknowledgment is made to Alfred A. Knopf, an imprint of the Knopf Doubleday Publishing Group, a division of Penguin Random House LLC, and Harold Ober Associates for permission to reprint "Tired" from *The Collected Poems of Langston Hughes* by Langston Hughes, edited by Arnold Rampersad with David Roessel, associate editor, copyright © 1951 by the Langston Hughes Estate, copyright © 1994 by the Estate of Langston Hughes. Digital rights and rights throughout the United Kingdom are controlled by Harold Ober Associates. Used by permission of Alfred A. Knopf, an imprint of the Knopf Doubleday Publishing Group, a division of Penguin Random House LLC, and Harold Ober Associates. All rights reserved.

Library of Congress Cataloging-in-Publication Data
Names: Villodas, Rich, author.
Title: Good and beautiful and kind:
becoming whole in a fractured world / Rich Villodas.
Description: First edition. | Colorado Springs: WaterBrook, [2022] |
Includes bibliographical references.
Identifiers: LCCN 2021061658 | ISBN 9780525654438 (trade paperback) |
ISBN 9780525654421 (ebook)
Subjects: LCSH: Jesus Christ—Example. | Christian life.
Classification: LCC BT304.2 .V55 2022 | DDC 232.9/04—dc23/eng/20220203
LC record available at https://lccn.loc.gov/2021061658

Printed in the United States of America on acid-free paper

waterbrookmultnomah.com

2nd Printing

Book design by Elizabeth A. D. Eno

Most WaterBrook books are available at special quantity discounts
for bulk purchase for premiums, fundraising, corporate and
educational needs by organizations, churches, and businesses.
Special books or book excerpts also can be created to fit specific needs.
For details, contact specialmarketscms@penguinrandomhouse.com.

For my children, Karis and Nathan.
When I think about goodness, beauty,
and kindness, I see your faces.

I am so tired of waiting,
Aren't you,
For the world to become good
And beautiful and kind?
Let us take a knife
And cut the world in two—
And see what worms are eating
At the rind.

—Langston Hughes, "Tired"

FOREWORD

BY ANN VOSKAMP

"There's a reason he called us his Body and not his Estate."
That's what Tib Pearson told me—Tib with his Red Wing
work boots and worn John Deere hat and hands weathered
and etched like a graying cedar rail.

"A Body is connected with sinew and veins, but an Estate is divided with fences and lines." He said it with his
hands, the way a man of the land does, and you could see
how his hands knew rusted wire and gnarled barbs and how
to free things caught in fences.

"You gotta cut down the fences—or you cut up the
Body."

It was Christ himself who gave us a mandate at the Last
Supper:

A new command I give you: Love one another. As
I have loved you, so you must love one another.

> By this everyone will know that you are my disci-
> ples, if you love one another. (John 13:34–35)

But the way we live that? How often do we take the mandate to love one another and make it some flimsy, take-it-or-leave-it suggestion?

Sometimes you'd think Christ's own were known by who they avoid, who they disdain, who they call out, who they label. You'd think being known by your love is being known as a liberal or conservative instead of a *Christian,* and there are a thousand things backward about this.

There was also Jesus before Calvary, Christ crushed beneath that Cross, Jesus begging that prayer of Maundy Thursday:

> My prayer is not for them alone. I pray also for
> those who will believe in me through their mes-
> sage . . . that they may be one as we are one—I in
> them and you in me—so that they may be
> brought to complete unity. Then the world will
> know that you sent me and have loved them even
> as you have loved me. (John 17:20, 22–23)

Think about these words. Only those who love are sent by Christ. Without love, Christ didn't send you.

It is no secret that we find ourselves living in some of the most divided and difficult times in many decades. Sometimes we feel like every headline brings more hard news that breaks our hearts, and where do we turn, how do we turn? Disease. War. Unrest. Uncertainty. In the turmoil of these times, Christ's people have not been immune. In fact, we have often found ourselves faced, as if in a mirror, with dramatic failures in loving like Jesus, exactly when circumstances around us have most demanded it. We have struggled as a community of faith, and many of us have faced feelings of betrayal or confusion. Discouragement is natural. Despair is tempting. But what are we to do to find a new way forward?

That is the large, quiet question behind the book you are holding in your hands. Rich Villodas is one of the deepest, wisest thinkers in the church today; his heart is shaped like the Cross and he speaks the dialect of Jesus—and sketches a real way forward. Rich speaks countercultural truths in a way that changes more than culture; it turns hearts. Rich is a man who doesn't say what tickling ears want to hear but who does say what actual hearts are desperate to know in times like these, because this is a man who lives with his heart pressed close to Christ's. And it is Christ's heart you will encounter on every page.

As you read these compelling words, keep a pen in hand and then write down your own words, in the margins, in a journal, because these pages are drawing a pathway to the good, the beautiful, the kind. You will want to trace the way, engage it, listen to the Holy Spirit beckoning and convicting and moving. And you will need to leave your own ink tracks to the good and beautiful and kind that you are seeking. Read with attentiveness because attentiveness is the beginning of receptiveness. And this is a book that you fully want to receive—these words will profoundly reorient.

As you begin the book, ask your own soul, *What would my life be like if I lived this way? Who will keep Jesus's com-*

*mandment, the mandate to love, and who will be the answer
to Christ's prayers? Who will love as he loved and live out the
good, the beautiful, the kind?*

The body of Christ has a thousand fractures and divi-
sions and circles, but obedience to the law of love is the
most expedient way to preach the gospel. Love is the most
radically subversive activism of all, the only thing that ever
changed anyone.

We never have to be afraid to love. As if love might gag
truth? As if it could kill God? Love never negates truth.
Love never silences truth. Love is the very *foundation* of
truth. Without love, truth crashes, a clanging cymbal. Without love, Christ didn't send you. Love is the language of
truth, and grace is the dialect of God, and truth is only
understandable if spoken with understanding love.

Christ prayed that mandate on Maundy Thursday, that
we might be brought to complete unity. That unity doesn't
mean we paper over our differences. It means we open the
papers of his Word and dialogue, not open fire and destroy.
True, there is always this tension between practicing unity
and preaching truth. But it is the tension of two people
hanging fiercely on to each other, like the tension of a
bridge, that the gospel might go forth into all the world.
We cannot let go of each other.

See, Tib Pearson knows what every farmer knows. If you
want a field to yield crops, you must sometimes tear down
fences.

That's how the enemy tries to cut the Body: If you disagree with someone on one point, then you must disdain or
dismiss them entirely. And if you acknowledge or affirm
someone, then you must agree with them entirely. This is a
lie. *Break it.*

Christ carries his Cross, and this is the call of God in this hour to the body of Christ in this world: Instead of drawing dividing lines in the community of Cross believers, the broken are called to demolish the walls of division.

We could be the people seeking the good, the beautiful, the kind, who are ready to obey the mandate of the Thursday before Good Friday: to find one person different than we are, and we broken people start breaking down walls by reaching out to someone of a different denomination, a different political leaning, a different nationality, a different culture, a different orientation, a different skin color, a different religion.

We could be the people seeking the good, the beautiful, the kind, who take seriously enough the Maundy Thursday commandment to actually *love* one another that we invite someone to our table from the other side of the fence.

And if there's someone we wouldn't want at our table, then we need to see who Jesus wanted to sit beside at the Last Supper table. If Jesus can dip from the same bowl as Judas, we can share the same table, the same space, with anyone, with grace.

We could be the people seeking the good, the beautiful, the kind, who instead of waging attack on the *implicit* issues of another's faith life spend our lives openly encouraging an *explicit* faith in the living Christ.

We could be the people seeking the good, the beautiful, the kind, who know that "the only thing that counts is faith expressing itself through love" (Galatians 5:6). We could be the people who know not just in our cerebral synapses but in the chambers of our bravely pounding hearts that if we have right doctrine but have not love, we are nothing more than a clanging cymbal.

Instead of being part of the clanging cymbal, we get to grab our pens and turn these pages, as the rare and exceptional wisdom of Rich Villodas leads us into more wholeness in a fractured world.

And Rich shows us that the only barbs the body ever knows isn't the fracturing of more hostile, barbed wire fences but the barbed thorns pressed into Christ's brow as he shows each of us how to live the cruciform love of the good and beautiful and kind.

CONTENTS

INTRODUCTION

Goodness. Beauty. Kindness. Three things we long for; three signs of a life well lived; three realities of God's presence. Yet they remain words hard to live into in our world, as we are prone to seeing (and experiencing) their negation: evil, ugliness, meanness.

We exist in a world eating away at itself. A world fractured from within. A world aching for wholeness. Whether the fractures are related to politics, race, religion, public health, or sexuality—to name a few of the polarizing issues we feel daily—our lives are not often marked by love, goodness, beauty, and kindness but by reactivity, impatience, judgmentalism, violence, and the inability to hold space with one another.

We carry the stress of our fractured world in our bodies and in our relationships. Friendships that once were a bedrock of strength have dissolved into wastelands of disgust. Families who once gathered around tables have converted those tables into walls. Many who used to share life together now live under a cloud of suspicion toward those same people.

All of this makes me wonder, How did we get here? And, more important, How can we begin to envision something different? These are the two simple questions that are crying out in our streets, homes, and churches and deep in our souls. We long for the good life, a beautiful life, a kind life.

The fractures within and around us don't feel right because our souls desire bonds of belonging and belovedness. We were not made for the kind of antagonism that pervades our world. We were made in love, and for love, by a good, beautiful, and kind God.

Sadly, however, we find ourselves stuck. Most of us believe the only option before us is to fondly recall the memories of the past, lamenting that those days will never return. But what if there was a future? What if it were possible to find ourselves learning to love in such a way that heals? What if the pain we carry didn't have the last word? What if there were a way that made for peace, joy, and love? I believe there is such a way.

To understand and respond to the moment we are in requires us to ask ourselves a few questions: How do we find wholeness? How do we love well? What are the forces behind the fractures? What kind of spiritual formation do we need to embody? In sum, what does it mean to have our lives formed by God's love? These are the questions I've been sitting with for many years—questions we will explore together.

I pastor a large, diverse, and complicated urban congregation, and the fractures of the world have often touched our lives. I have had to be formed—and do my best to form others—in the way of love, in the way of Jesus. The diversity we treasure—along racial, generational, economic, political, and theological lines—has forced us to consistently reexamine our commitment to the way of Christ's kingdom. I have repeatedly learned that it's much easier to preach the kingdom than to live it. As a community, we have had to rediscover the truth that wholeness, healing, and love are found in the ancient path of Jesus.

Jesus offers a way of being human that is powerful enough to tear down the walls of hostility we have grown accustomed to. His gospel gives us a vision of loving well. It's a soul-healing, enemy-reconciling, truth-telling, justice-embodying, sin-conquering vision. It's one we can't live without, especially since most people have not been formed to love well in our society, including within our churches.

It's easy to see how love—personally and publicly—feels elusive. But what if that could change? What if we submitted ourselves to an ancient path that forms us out of sentimentality and into self-giving love, out of anger and into compassion, out of fear and into hospitality? This is the essence of this book.

To talk about big words like *wholeness, goodness, beauty, kindness,* and *love* is no small task. The best wordsmiths have stammered trying to succinctly articulate these signs of the divine. My attempt in this book is oriented around not so much defining them as describing them and then offering a pathway toward them.

CUTTING THE WORLD IN TWO

To arrive at this point, however, requires us to do the hard work of looking within. It's something like the work the

American poet Langston Hughes exhorted us to do in his
timeless poem "Tired":

> I am so tired of waiting,
> Aren't you,
> For the world to become good
> And beautiful and kind?
> Let us take a knife
> And cut the world in two—
> And see what worms are eating
> At the rind.[1]

After naming the longing we all have for a world marked
by goodness, beauty, and kindness, Hughes abruptly ad-
monishes us to take a knife and "cut the world in two" to
examine the realities beneath the surface. It's a vivid image.
It's important to note that he is not recommending a dualistic, judgmental way of life where we establish who's in and
who's out. It is not the language of division but of depth.
He is trying to help us look deeper—to examine the rot and
the worms eating away at our lives. Hughes knew that it's
only when we start here that we can truly undertake a life of
goodness, beauty, and kindness. That's where I'd like to
take you as well. I don't want to cut the world in two just
to fixate on the worms. You can go to social media for that.
Rather, I want you to see the worms that often go unno-
ticed and then offer a vision of what we can become if we
allow God to work in and through us.

As we journey together, we will walk through three parts
to root us in this way of life. In the first part, we will "cut
the world in two," exploring the ways that love, goodness,
beauty, and kindness get *eaten from* our lives and our world.

We'll navigate the themes of sin, powers and principalities, and trauma.

In the second part, we will focus on how the good, beautiful, and kind life gets *formed* in us through contemplative prayer, humility, and the cultivation of calm presence.

The final part will examine the ways all this gets *embodied* through healthy conflict, forgiveness, and justice.

Before we examine these themes, a word about patience is in order. Living a good, beautiful, and kind life—the way of Christ's love—is not something that happens overnight. Love is a fruit of the Holy Spirit; that is to say, it grows slowly. There is no shortcut to love. The assumption that many carry is that God can produce something in us quickly, but fruit is grown over time. The gifts of the Spirit are given generously and quickly. Not so with the fruit of the Spirit. One of the dangers is we expect the gifts of the Spirit to quickly do what only the fruit of the Spirit is meant to do slowly.

So give yourself grace. We are all on the journey. If we try to rush through this content, we will have merely read a book, not opened ourselves to the work of God's grace. But this work is too important to skim by. As you read, take notes in the margins. Underline and highlight generously. Journal and find a friend or a group to process your findings with. The best kind of transformation happens in community.

With all that, let's pursue the good and beautiful and kind life together.

Lord, you desire us to be formed by your love. Give us grace not to live this material perfectly but to wrestle with it faithfully. By the end of the journey, may we have moved closer to you, our neighbor, and ourselves. In Jesus's name, amen.

PART ONE

THE FORCES BEHIND
THE FRACTURES

CHAPTER 1

A FAILURE TO LOVE

Sin, the Fracturing of Reality

At its core, sin is failure to love. It's a power that "curves us inward." In the words of North African bishop Saint Augustine, humanity is *incurvatus in se,* curved in on itself.[1] Humanity suffers from a severe condition. No matter if our physical eyes may be able to gaze upward, our spiritual vision tends to curve horribly in upon itself. And with this stunting self-focus of our attention, we cut out love.

Not many of us associate sin with love. Sin usually conjures images of lawbreaking, trespassing, and debt (all helpful metaphors for understanding our relationship to God). What I would like to propose, however, is that we broaden our scope—or rather, focus our lens. We must understand sin in the light of love as we seek to live in the way of Jesus, especially those of us who long for wholeness.

When Jesus was asked what the greatest commandment is, he responded with absolute clarity: *Love.* Love is the greatest command. He said, " 'Love the Lord your God with all your heart and with all your soul and with all your mind.' This is the first and greatest commandment. And the second is like it: 'Love your neighbor as yourself.' All the Law and the Prophets hang on these two commandments" (Matthew 22:37–40).

Jesus's summary of Holy Scripture leads me to a conclusion that might surprise you: If the greatest commandment given by Jesus is rooted in love, the greatest sin—and perhaps all sin—must in some way be the rejection of this command. This is what makes sin so pernicious. It orients us inward. It curves us in on ourselves, and in so doing, it uproots love, goodness, beauty, and kindness.

To classify sin as failure to love is not to sentimentalize or soften it. It's to frame the very essence of our lives with God and one another in the way Jesus did. The chief end of humanity is "to glorify God, and to enjoy him forever,"[2] to paraphrase the old Westminster Catechism. And the means to this end is simple: love. Love is the fulfillment of faith; sin is the negation of it.

Paul the apostle captured this better than anyone besides Jesus himself. In the early years of the church, new communities were being formed, often in ways that somehow sidelined love. Because of a variety of temptations, failures, and distractions, love was not regarded as the most important expression of faith. As one example, among some Christ followers in the city of Corinth (in ancient Greece), love was superseded by charisma. This emphasis resulted in many interpersonal fractures, which led Paul to write a letter to them. As he neared the end of his correspondence, he wrote what has become famously known as the "love chapter." First Corinthians 13 shows up in almost every wedding ceremony. It's a beautiful description of what love is: "patient," "kind," and all the rest. But it's important to note that Paul didn't have wedding bells, bridesmaids, and bouquets in mind when he wrote the passage. It was not intended to give the reader warm, fuzzy feelings. The chapter was Paul's word of rebuke to Christ followers who had become fractured and distracted. They were marked by great miracles and charisma among them, but they had little of maturity and character where it counted.

To end the chapter, Paul made it plain: "And now these three remain: faith, hope and love. But the greatest of these is love" (verse 13). If love is the greatest good, sin must be the antithesis of it. Sin is not just a violation of a law; it's the disruption of love.

It might be easy to think of this as simply an abstract theological idea. But what if it wasn't? What if you could trace all the horribly concrete wounds and fractures of our culture, churches, families, and most intimate relationships to the disruption of love? What if our world—so far from being good, beautiful, or kind—was in the state it was in precisely because of this failure to love?

RECOVERING "SIN"

Now, the last thing you might want right now is another preacher pointing out sin. *Here goes Rich, lecturing on morality—in the first chapter, no less!* If that's you, please give me a chance, because I want us to understand together what Langston Hughes called the "worms . . . eating at the rind." And we cannot do so, we cannot name or understand the forces that sabotage our lives and break our society's most sacred bonds if we lack an intimate, accurate understanding of both love and sin.

The historical and modern fractures in our world need a

category vast enough to make sense of our vast present pain. We need sociology and psychology to help us understand our fractures, but it is *theology* that places them in their true and larger context. It might sound strange to say this, but we need sin. We can't talk about ourselves or our society accurately without it.

In her book *Speaking of Sin,* Episcopal priest Barbara Brown Taylor noted that

> abandoning the language of sin will not make sin go away. Human beings will continue to experience alienation, deformation, damnation, and death no matter what we call them. Abandoning the language will simply leave us speechless before them, and increase our denial of their presence in our lives.[3]

In a culture where Christianity is no longer the center of human reflection and engagement in the world, any talk of sin can be rough sledding. Sin has come to be associated with judgmentalism, bigotry, and a selective, inconsistent moralism, leading people—religious or otherwise—to conclude that it's just another word used to control and coerce people in a particular way. As a pastor, I must admit that there is much truth in this. Sin as a concept *has* been abused, used to control, and used to shelter and even justify indefensible hypocrisy by spiritual communities in our shared social life.

Recently, I had a conversation with a neighbor in my apartment building. After hearing that I was a pastor, he began to wax eloquent about the oppressive tendencies of religion. For him, *sin* has been a manipulative word to keep people in line—to control their sexuality, money, and political convictions. It implies a threat. In his opinion, sin is just another way to create a world in the image of the powerful or privileged. As he shared this, I had to agree with much of what he was saying. Just look around! The language of sin has been used as a hammer to crush anyone who doesn't share the same ethical standards, and that's tragic. But there are more redemptive ways of understanding sin. And holding fast the hope that we can learn to love in a way that restores, shouldn't we try to do so?

REFRAMING SIN

When we define sin relative to love, we do not have to discard outright the traditional ways we have understood sin. In fact, there are clear biblical passages we can point to that speak of sin as breaking God's law. But they do not present a complete picture, and most of us need a course correction. In our culture, sin has usually not been seen as a failure to love but almost exclusively as a violation of a law: God's law.

When we expand our understanding, we can better assess our spiritual health. Perhaps we have not broken God's law today, in a strictly defined legal sense. But have we failed to love? Have we curved in on ourselves, missing opportunities to share the love of Christ with the poor or vulnerable around us? Very likely, and it is this increased standard of difficulty that Christ so memorably calls us to embrace. Remember the Sermon on the Mount? Again and again, Jesus quoted the Law of Moses in Matthew 5: "You have heard that it was said . . ." and then reframed the teaching according to love with "But I tell you . . ." We still live under the difficult inspiration of that iconic teaching today.

A robust theology of sin helps us live beyond self-deception. A limited theology of sin often results in a false sense of spiritual maturity. Like the Pharisee in one of Christ's parables, who looked around in pride and thanked God that he wasn't like *those* sinners (see Luke 18:11), it is a small step from a narrow understanding of sin straight into the depths of it. In other words, it's easy to think, *Well, I'm not doing* that, *so I must be okay*. But sin is not just about "not doing that." Sin is the negation of love.

When spiritual vitality is measured by sin-avoidance, we deceive ourselves into thinking that we are following Jesus faithfully. But following Jesus is to be measured by love— love for God expressed in love for neighbor. This is the good, beautiful, and kind life. It took me some years to realize this. In fact, I need to be reminded of it often.

When I became a Christian as a twenty-year-old, I was touched by the hope found in the love of God. I heard a preacher proclaim the good news that God cared about my past, present, and future and wanted to rescue me from sin. I received this news with joy and surrendered my life to Jesus. But upon my entry into life with Christ, sin was overwhelmingly presented as violation of a moral code. And as a result, holiness was understood with a similar negativity: as sin-avoidance. Sin was privatized. Confession meant admitting to someone the deep, dark secrets of my soul (and maybe my internet search history). There was little if any connection to seeing love as the repudiation of sin. Instead, sin was the things we did in private, usually things of which we were ashamed.

Of course, God is concerned about every facet of our

lives, including our private lives, down to their most intimate aspects. The invitation to follow Jesus must extend to
the moments when we are alone and the decisions we make
there. But the gravitational pull in many sectors of Christianity is to spend most of our time focused on our private
lives. Sin, functionally, is an activity done in secret.

In my early days as a follower of Christ, I found myself
obsessed with sin-avoidance. Spiritual victory was found in
not looking at porn (such a low bar for holiness). I took
inventory of the music I listened to, the movies I watched,
and the company I kept. If I sensed that any of these things
would lead me into sin, I did my best to cut it out. On one
hand, this sounds like good discipline. But if this is the sole,
or even primary, way of understanding sin, we will find ourselves functioning as disciples of the devil. Let me explain.

In his book *New Seeds of Contemplation*, poet and theologian Thomas Merton observed the way we function as the
devil's disciples:

> The devil makes many disciples by preaching
> against sin. He convinces them of the great evil of
> sin, induces a crisis of guilt by which "God is sat-
> isfied," and after that he lets them spend the rest
> of their lives meditating on the intense sinfulness
> and evident reprobation of other men.[4]

In other words, by becoming solely focused on abstain-
ing from sin (defined very narrowly), we live by a crushing
moralism that robs us from enjoying God and self-righteously
places us above others. This is one of the sad expressions of
Christian faith we witness, or perhaps even perpetuate in
our own lives.

Because this tends to be the direction of much of our faith, Christianity is regarded as a hypocritical religion by the watching world. The world sees the scrupulosity around individual sin and personal piety without the corresponding commitment to love and justice. When people berate Christians for a lack of love, they demonstrate that they understand the tenets of faith very well. Christianity is about the love of God being expressed through followers of Jesus. It sometimes seems as if the world knows more about our faith than we do. This assessment of Christianity is not the full story, of course. We can't understand much of the goodness of the world we inhabit without the love of Christians over many centuries. But humility is important here. In fact, Jesus had some strong words for religious leaders in his day around this matter:

> Woe to you, teachers of the law and Pharisees, you hypocrites! You give a tenth of your spices— mint, dill and cumin. But you have neglected the more important matters of the law—justice, mercy and faithfulness. You should have practiced the latter, without neglecting the former. (Matthew 23:23)

Listen closely! Jesus didn't dismiss the personal expressions of faith from religious people who offered God 10 percent of their spices (which was Jesus's way of noting how meticulous they were in following the Law). But Jesus called out the hypocrisy of doing so without the corresponding commitment to love. They followed the law but forsook love.

This brings us to an important aspect of understanding

the way sin works. It is a power that turns us inward and seeks to keep us there, which is why we are so fractured, internally and externally. How can one who has become locked into their own soul expect to cultivate a healthy relationship with the wider world?

TURNED INWARD

There is great value in looking inward. Interior examination is a commitment we all must give ourselves to, through God's grace. But note that his grace turns us inward for the sake of self-awareness, confession, and ultimately love. This process, in the paradoxical beauty of God's way, ends with us growing in our outward love. Sin, however, turns us inward in such a way that we get stuck, horribly so. It causes us to desire an illusion—to center the world on our comfort, security, fear, desire, and personal perspective. It curves us inward, leaving little room for God or anyone else.

So, sin is not just something we do but a power we fall under, a power that curves us into ourselves until we become stuck there. Now once again, ask with me these age-old questions: Why is the world fractured? Why are we so broken? The simple answer is right here: sin. Its results are that we become closed off from others. Sin is destructive because it causes us to live self-seeking lives over and against others. It is never personal, never private. It's what's behind the subtle (and not-so-subtle) grasping for power that marks our world. It's the energy behind the violence, the dynamo beneath all the arrogance, apathy, and hatred.

Sin is at work when those who have experienced undeniable racism are not met with empathy and care but rather are demonized for naming the problem. Sin is what's at work when we shrug our shoulders in the face of grave injustice. Sin is present when we refuse to treat another with dignity. Sin exists when we injure another with our gossip. Sin is manifested—as we confess in prayer every week in our congregation—in what we have done and in what we have left undone. A story might help us here.

A LOVE THAT RESISTS *INCURVATUS IN SE*

Living into the eternal life that God promises comes as we give ourselves to the work of love. Eternal life is granted to us by God's free grace, but living into it requires love-saturated lives—love that resists the gravity of *incurvatus in se*.

There's a beloved story Jesus told that has shaped imaginations for thousands of years. It's found in the tenth chapter of Luke's gospel, about a good Samaritan. One day, Jesus was asked how eternal life could be inherited. Once again, he responded with "love" as the way—love for God, and love for one's neighbor.

Jesus told the story of a man who was beaten and left for dead on the road. In his cast of characters, first a priest came along, followed by a Levite (a significant religious leader with the "ideal" social and ethnic pedigree). The two were seemingly on their way to a worship gathering and made no attempt to help this beaten man. But then onto the scene came a Samaritan—an unlikely hero for the audience Jesus was addressing.

But when the Samaritan saw the beaten man, he took pity on him. He went to him and bandaged his wounds, pouring on oil and wine. Then he put the man on his own donkey, brought him to an inn, and took care of him. The next day, he took out two denarii and gave them to the innkeeper. " 'Look after him,' he said, 'and when I return, I will reimburse you for any extra expense you may have' " (verse 35).

There's no talk of sin in this story, but we can infer something important: The person who resisted *incurvatus in se* was the Samaritan. In his compassion, advocacy, and generosity, he didn't turn inward. He gave himself to love—love for God expressed in love for neighbor. Ironically, the religious leaders who knew all the Bible verses about sin were turned in on themselves.

I read this story with fear and trembling, as I was reminded that I can live a so-called morally upright life and still be caught in sin, turning inward. To be caught in sin is usually understood in terms of addictive behavior. But again, let's broaden our approach. We are also caught in sin when we fail to love. This is what the first few stories in the Bible describe.

STORIES OF TURNING INWARD

I love a good origin story. It has a way of filling the gaps in knowledge that helps us better understand the heroes we've come to love or the villains we've come to despise. That's what the opening pages of Genesis do, not just for an individual but for the entire human race. In these stories, particularly the ones in the first eleven chapters, our collective origin story is told.

The tendency to turn inward—which we all have—is

what makes this world bound to sin. Sin separates us from loving communion with God and with others. This has been the story from the very beginning. A cursory look at three stories in the first eleven chapters of Genesis demonstrates this reality. As we study these stories, we will find ourselves in them.

Adam and Eve: Turning Inward Through Grasping

Adam and Eve are tempted by the idea of being like God, knowing good from evil. By this they are enticed to take on what is only God's prerogative: determining what is good from what is evil. More than being made in God's image, they wanted to *be* God. Instead of looking outward and upward for their definitions of right, good, and truth, they looked within, succumbing to a form of grasping, of spiritual greed.

The story follows them, in their greed, from temptation to fall. It is an eternal story. Humans have followed suit ever since. Before that infamous moment of eating the fruit from the tree, they enjoyed loving communion with God. They were naked and unashamed. They lived joyfully free in the presence of the Lord. But as the story goes, their gaze turned inward. At the Serpent's prompting, they pondered the power they could have if they ate from the tree.

To begin with, the tree signified a holy limit. God had placed before them a boundary that was both necessary and out of his love. But soon enough, in the presence of temptation, it became, in the words of Tolkien's magic ring–obsessed character Gollum, "my precious." Desiring the fruit, rationalizing their situation, and ultimately eating from the tree of the knowledge of good and evil was a result of sin turning them inward. By the time they sank their teeth into the fruit, love had already been uprooted. And this turning inward has continued ever since.

Whether the grasping comes in the form of taking land and calling it manifest destiny, whether it's corporations seizing land and exploiting the environment for economic self-interests and calling it innovation, or whether it comes in the form of sexual abuse or in the workaholism that fractures our families, our world is caught in the sinful trap of aggressive grasping. We turn inward through grasping.

Cain and Abel: Turning Inward Through Envy

At the beginning of Genesis 4, Adam and Eve made love and had a son. Then they had another. All seemed to be going well with "the Addams family." (See what I did there? It's okay to groan.) I imagine the doting parents. If they were living today, they'd have been taking family portraits, dressing themselves with white tops and khakis. They have a cooing baby on each lap as they grin wide and say cheese. So much life and joy.

Even though they were removed from the garden, they were a family. But then things began to change. The story of sin started with a man and a woman and continued as it was passed down to siblings—a farmer (Cain) and a shepherd (Abel).

As we read on in Genesis, we soon see that the two brothers were very different. Their differences are depicted in their worship. When Abel offered sacrifices, he gave the firstfruits—the very best—and the smoke would go up. This was not Cain's approach. The story says that God was more pleased with Abel's offering, which led to Cain becoming angry and envious. Cain's jealousy turned him inward, leaving him to conclude that only one person could be a success: him or his brother. That simple. The happy family's collapse began with a fracture that happened inwardly, though soon it was to have bloody outward consequences.

Few of us admit to being envious. Jealousy is too petty a thing to feel proud about, something beneath our dignity. Yet jealousy is one of the most pervasive and destructive forces on the planet and more deeply ingrained in all of us than we usually have the courage to admit.

Here's the thing about envy: We are often envious about only the things that matter most to us. Jealousy reveals the idols of our hearts. For example, I'm a preacher and a writer. When I see someone playing an instrument with skill and beauty, I don't have one envious bone in my body. I admire and receive the gift. Why? Because I'm not a musician. However, when I see another preacher enjoying success or praise, especially someone about my age, I'm not usually enraptured with delight. All too often, my first small and sinful response is envy.

Now, the first "noticing" here is not always bad. But you know you've crossed the line and are on the verge of coveting when the intense longing that often comes from comparison with another person (*I want what they have / to be what they are*) does not help you give thanks or live with more wholeness in your life but rather leads to greater levels of dissatisfaction and disconnection from what you already have. Moreover, it leads to you participating in the most damaging "game" out there: the zero-sum game.

The zero-sum game is at the core of much of our social interactions. It would have us believe that for *me* to truly win, *you* need to unequivocally lose. This is the nature of political life and the consumer market. The goal in life is not to succeed but to prosper in such a way that clearly delineates me from you. Competition gives birth to conquest; success requires another's elimination. This is at the heart of a world that fails to love well.

Cain's envy produced an imaginary world. That "paradise" could exist only if his brother was eliminated from it. This sin—trying to make outward reality resemble our stunted, cramped inward one—has repeated through the ages. It's the source of our fractured existence, whether through the ethnic cleansings of the Rohingya people in Myanmar, the political animus that feeds off the defeat of one's opponent, or the private desires we harbor for others to fail for us to look good. This way of living marks us—like it did Cain. The "paradise" we thought we'd find never materializes.

The Tower of Babel:
Turning Inward Through Exclusionism

The final story of turning inward we'll examine relates to the Tower of Babel. By the time we get to this story in Genesis 11, we see how humanity has continued to go its own way, following the tragic trajectory of Adam, Eve, and Cain. The people are said to have been going east (the symbolic direction Adam and Eve were sent after being expelled from Eden, pointing to their distance from God) to build a tower. On the surface, this seems innocent enough. Why is God concerned? It's a tower! As we know, there is no structure that could be built that can take over heaven. God's dwelling place is in a different dimension of reality.

Even so, God saw their efforts as dangerous. One of the

reasons they wanted to build a city and this tower was because they were afraid of being scattered throughout the
earth (see verse 4).

So, what's the problem? Why is it wrong to want to stay
put? It's a good question. The answer is found in God's
commission for them to fill the earth. Earlier in Genesis
(1:28), God gave his people the mandate to fill the earth, to
show forth his presence throughout the earth. The problem
with them building this city is they would rather stay within
their homogeneous setting than have their lives intersect
with others. Collectively and geographically, they turned inward. Rather than going in faith, they began to stay in pride.

God saw the deep problems this way of life produces.
They lived in fear of those who were different, so they created a tower. I read this as a bubble. An echo chamber. The
problem with their brand of unity is that it would lead to
uniformity, and uniformity has a way of producing exclusiv-
ity and hierarchies—something we see reenacted daily in
expressions of Christian nationalism, racism, ethnocentrism,
and sexism. It's seen in the ways social media, through its
sophisticated algorithms, turns us in on ourselves. It's expressed in the toxicity of political power plays. While the
trappings of such fractures are new, the deeper issue is not.

The "towers" we build are often rooted in the idolatry
of self-interest. Whether it comes in the form of "class towers" that separate us from the poor, or "technological towers" that keep us connected to those who see and believe all
the things we do, sin has a way of absolutizing our values
(especially the ones that were never intended to be absolute) in ways that cause greater fragmentation. In the words
of family systems theorist Edwin Friedman, our society is
marked by a "herding instinct,"[5] where the forces for to-

getherness triumph over all. The question becomes, *Am I building a tower (that is, a life) that turns me in on myself?* If I am, I'm in spiritual danger.

UNCURVING OURSELVES

Grasping. Envy. Exclusionism. Our collective origin story, seen in the first part of the first book of the Bible, is marked by these realities. They remind us that sin is not just something we do but a power we are under, a power turning us inward, but inward in the wrong way.

This leads to an important question: How do we "uncurve" ourselves? To be uncurved is to be rooted in love, orienting our lives toward the good, beautiful, and kind lives God dreams for us, but the task sounds insurmountable. And it is insurmountable. For *us*. The weight of sin presses us inward. We are caught under its oppressive power.

The world apart from God is in sin, and we can't rescue ourselves. We can't save ourselves. We can't work or legislate our way out of it. We can't educate ourselves out of its grip. We don't overcome it through progressive achievements or by moral consistency. The antidote for sin is not found by looking to the left or the right. It's in a power outside of ourselves: the Cross of Christ.

Christian faith compels us to say in one breath that a fragmenting power is at work within each of us and between all of us, and in the next breath announce that there's a way out. As the Swiss theologian Karl Barth said, "The reality of sin cannot be known or described except in relation to the One who has vanquished it."[6] In other words, whenever we talk about sin, it's a good practice to immediately announce that it has been overcome by Christ. This is the good news!

The gospel is the good news that God's kingdom has come near in Jesus Christ, and through his life, death, resurrection, and enthronement, the powers of sin and death no longer have the last word. On the cross and in his resurrection, Jesus took on sin. The sin that has ravaged our personal lives. The sin that has been the source of so much heartache throughout history. The sin that requires unequivocal judgment. Jesus conquered it. In his so doing, we are forgiven through his blood and empowered by the Spirit to live in loving union with God and with our neighbor, anticipating the fullness of our union with the triune God at the end of history. This good news is to free us from the inward turn. The weight of sin has been carried on the shoulders of Jesus, and his Spirit animates our lives, "uncurving" us every day.

Later in this book, we will explore further how this process becomes embodied in us, but for now, a brief word about a significant spiritual practice is in order. For those who trust in Jesus's finished work on the cross, we have the great joy of living within his love. As we open ourselves to God's presence, his love orients us in a new direction held steady by one of the most important spiritual practices in the Christian life: confession.

THE PRACTICE OF CONFESSION OF SIN

Confession uncurves us. If we believe that sin has been handled definitively in Christ and that the full victory over it will occur when he fully renews the world, what do we do in the meantime? There are many good answers to this question, but I doubt you'll find a better starting point than confession.

Until we consistently live from a place of humility, confessing our sins before God and one another, we will find ourselves gradually turning inward. This is why we need the wisdom of Barbara Brown Taylor, who provocatively said that sin is our only hope. What she meant by this is that "when we see how we have turned away from God, then and only then do we have what we need to begin turning back. *Sin is our only hope,* the fire alarm that wakes us up to the possibility of true repentance."[7]

Followers of Christ establish our moral credibility in the world by routinely and fearlessly confessing and repenting of sin. And we lose our credibility by refusing to name our sins. This is the paradox of faith. To confess our sins doesn't mean obsessing over our mistakes. To confess our sins—especially together in a community—is an act of solidarity. It's a practice reminding us that we are all on equal footing, all in need of grace; that we all have sinned and have been sinned against; that we are in the same broken family.

Every Sunday in our worship at New Life Fellowship Church, we take a moment to recall the previous week in the silence of our hearts. We name our failures and shortcomings and then confess aloud a prayer that ties us together in our weaknesses. Whenever the Lenten season comes around, we observe Ash Wednesday. It's the annual reminder that we are far more weak, frail, broken, and marked by sin than we think. It's also the reminder that God is far more gracious, merciful, present, and loving than we can believe.

This practice of confession in our worship gatherings

frees us to confess our sins the other six days of the week. When we scold our children in ways that harm them, confession forms in us the humility to ask for their pardon. When after a heated exchange with someone that leads to wounding words, we limit sin's power by confessing our carelessness and requesting grace from the person. That is how the world moves toward wholeness—not by our covering up our sins and mistakes, but by lovingly acknowledging them before God and one another. This is the starting point for a good and beautiful and kind life.

And yet the call to this kind of life has another dimension we must pay attention to. The world is not just fractured because we turn inward. It's fractured because of an unseen enemy. And this enemy is legion.

CHAPTER 2

THE UNSEEN ENEMY

Living Against the Powers

There she was. A dutiful, churchgoing, apple pie–making mom from Texas. She was known in the neighborhood for her sweet Southern hospitality, ready to encourage someone at a moment's notice with a verse from the Bible. She never uttered a curse word in her life, having memorized and taken seriously the passage that says, "Do not let any unwholesome talk come out of your mouths" (Ephesians 4:29). She always had a smile on her face, leading many people to wonder about her joyful disposition. "How are you so happy?" the neighbors always asked. Like clockwork, this godly mom replied, "Don't be silly, dear. Christians are called to rejoice in the Lord, always, and again I say, rejoice."

On a hot summer day, this dutiful Christian invited some friends over for lunch to talk about the latest news in the neighborhood church. She didn't gather them for idle talk but rather to genuinely pray—to commit their town and neighbors to the things of God. She and her husband had worked hard to raise their children in the ways of the Lord.

They were financially generous and prayed before bed, before meals, and before long car rides. This family was the model of Christian goodness.

One day the family learned of an interesting community gathering. They were always looking for a moment to bond and to create memories. This night would be no different. The entire community, it seemed, would gather in the local park to celebrate, fellowship, and witness an event familiar to many in the South. You see, Jesse Washington, a Black seventeen-year-old, would be lynched that night.[1]

More than ten thousand people—including civic leaders, children, police officers, and "good" religious people—would gather to watch this public execution. James Cone, in his book *The Cross and the Lynching Tree*, noted that "in its heyday, the lynching of black Americans was no secret. It was a public spectacle, often announced in advance in newspapers and over radios, attracting crowds of up to twenty thousand people."[2] Lynchings would make their way onto postcards that were then mailed to friends across the nation with smiling faces in the foreground of the card and hanging bodies in the background.

The mom mentioned above could have been any mom on that day. In fact, in that part of Texas and in many other states, it was *many* moms, and dads—and, painfully, children too. When I think of this level of brutality and dehumanization mixed with a bewildering spirit of joyful celebration, I can arrive at only one conclusion: There's something else going on. Something sinister beyond what we can see.

How could this sweet, Bible-reading, pie-making, never-cursing mom bring her children to witness this abhorrent "family-friendly" act of evil? How did she reconcile her faith with this morally despicable act? Well, in many ways, there was nothing to reconcile. Lynching was as American as apple pie. Even with the Lord's Prayer on her lips, she was deceived by an insidious power greater than herself.

In the first chapter, we explored the ways sin, like the worms in Hughes's poem, eats away love, goodness, beauty, and kindness. To be born into this world means that we are all under a power that would have us live *incurvatus in se:* curved inward. But the problem we face is not located simply within our hearts. There is something else at work that we often fail to see but must begin to pay attention to.

We are so accustomed to clear, easy answers when it comes to pointing out what's wrong with the world. (It's the Liberals! The Conservatives! The people who put pineapple on their pizza!) But the biblical narrative helps us acknowledge that finding the source of the problem is more complicated than we think.

In the biblical story, there are forces outside ourselves somehow wreaking havoc in our lives, seducing us away from the God of love. Those forces are known as—to use biblical terms—powers and principalities. They refer to the belief held by the writers of the Bible, including the prophet Daniel and the apostle Paul, that behind the actions of people and groups of people (including nations, churches, and institutions) there exist spiritual forces whose agenda runs counter to the way of God.

I'm fully mindful that to make intellectual room for this kind of outside force might be difficult for some. We like to think that we are self-aware and smart enough to recognize when we are being influenced by forces outside of or larger than ourselves. We might also think we are strong enough to resist any outside influence. And that sense of insight and strength is exactly the problem. We are more vulnerable and exposed than we think.

POWERS AND PRINCIPALITIES

The whole world is spiritual, but it usually does a good job hiding it. Have you ever watched the news, read the paper, or scrolled through social media and wondered how it was possible that certain evils were possible, let alone seen as "good" by certain people? Have you ever had the feeling that something else was operating behind the scenes? When I come across stories of child abuse, senseless war, or the vicious, often violent ways people relate to those who don't hold similar views, I can't help but wonder if there is more to the story than we first see. Could it be that we are being pushed and prodded by something sinister in these situations that seem to go beyond the logic or limits of everyday human depravity? If you feel that way, you're not alone. In fact, this feeling just might be pointing to an unseen enemy whose sole purpose is to cut us off from love.

Now, I'm not talking about conspiracy theories. I'm not looking for a demon under every rock. I'm not ascribing to an oversimple or underthought view of the world. But this I believe: We can't understand the fragmentation we experience without expanding our language for the forces that fill the world and influence us. This is one place where Scripture comes in handy—in giving categories large enough to understand the evil that is curving the world (and our own hearts) in on itself.

Powers and *principalities* are not terms we use every day. In fact, they can be quite foreign and strange. My wife,

Rosie, reminded me recently of the first time she heard these words in church, as a teenager. One day her Sunday school teacher mentioned that the battle we wage is against powers and principalities, to which Rosie's young friend curiously asked, "Who's the Prince of Palities?"

For some people, powers are seen as individual evil spirits wreaking havoc inside individuals. Movies like *The Exorcist* come to mind. For others, powers are metaphorical language to explain institutional sin. In some Christian traditions, the notion of powers and principalities is plain to see—the singular way to understand problems, oftentimes in a context of worship. I've been at quite a few Pentecostal and Charismatic gatherings where the sound system wasn't working and people started fervently rebuking Satan. (I mean, it *would* help to turn the sound system on, people.)

In other streams of faith, Christians are embarrassed to ever use the language of powers, demons, and Satan seriously. This language is replaced with either exclusive psychological explanation or with an emphasis on human progress. But as theologian Walter Wink noted,

> The utter failure of our optimistic views of progress to account for the escalating horrors of our time demands at least a fresh start at understanding the source and virulence of the evils that are submerging our age.[3]

What was he saying? That we can't begin to describe the fracturing evil of our time without spiritual language large enough to do so.

I want to make a case for us to urgently consider the presence of powers and principalities in ways we might not have before. In doing so, I hope to help us arrive at a much deeper level of understanding and thereby uproot the forces that lead us to greater fragmentation and instead be rooted in love. This is the urgent reality we must contend with: The problem with the world is not just "in us"; it's also "out there."

WHAT ARE THE POWERS?

To gain a full perspective on the powers, it's important to see how they are depicted in Scripture. Many people automatically equate powers with demons, but that's not the best connection. While the powers are influenced by demonic forces, they are not to be regarded as disembodied evil personalities, nor should they be considered solely as nefarious institutional structures. The powers need to be understood as the convergence of hostile spiritual forces hosted within individuals, systemic structures, and institutional structures. In this way, my definition of powers and principalities is as follows:

> Powers and principalities are spiritual forces that become hostile, taking root in individuals, ideologies, and institutions, with the goal of deception, division, and depersonalization.

It's important to note that the powers are not exclusively evil. They were established to function in a particular way, holding together life in obedience to God. The apostle Paul noted that the powers and principalities were created by

God to be stewarded for the well-being of all creation (see Colossians 1:15–17) and for his glory. As theologian Hendrik Berkhof wrote, "By no means does Paul think of the Powers as evil in themselves. They are the linkage between God's love and visible human experience. They are to hold life together, preserving it within God's love."[4]

One day these powers will be fully subjected to God's intention for all things, but in the meantime, they are rebellious and must be disarmed. This is one of the beautiful parts of the New Testament, which poetically describes how Christ has *already* disarmed the powers (see Colossians 2:15), but the task remains for us to continue to witness and live out this reality.

THE POWERS ARE DIVERSE

When you look at the horror in the world—from child abuse to genocide, from racism to terrorism, from addictions to exploitative capitalism—the powers and principalities are pervasive. They show up everywhere. Here's a short list of places they frequent:

- governments
- political leaders
- corporations
- churches
- denominations
- educational institutions
- cities
- nations

In the biblical view, the powers and principalities are both invisible and visible, heavenly and earthly, spiritual and institutional. All the powers mentioned in this list are not bad per se. But for various reasons, usually brought on by human idolatry (including the idolatrous lust for power and money), the powers become twisted and capable of taking over the lives of everyday people. This possession is manifested not through spinning heads and frightening shrieks but through the perpetuation of deception, division, and depersonalization. The powers, in this possessed state, influence those directly within their orbit, severely compromising even those who might be regarded as moral people, like the mom from Texas in the story I opened this chapter with. What else could explain the level of spiritual blindness and disconnection for a kind, mannerly, hospitable woman to witness the murder of a boy by her community, and to do so with no more pain to her conscience than she'd have attending a church picnic?

It's quite easy to focus on individual morality to the exclusion of larger forces. It's easy to painstakingly prioritize personal sins without engaging systemic injustice on a larger scale. Author and theologian James Cone poignantly captured this when he said, "While churches are debating whether a whale swallowed Jonah, the state is enacting inhuman laws against the oppressed."[5] How else to explain such disconnection, such spiritual blindness, than the operation of some powerful deception that moves social forces for twisted, spiritual ends?

In the process Cone described, Christians fail to live up to the conquering victory of Christ over the forces of the world. Because of this failure by God's people, the powers remain unchecked in our lives, organizations, cultures, and nations. We debate if they even exist, while all around us, the personal and systemic evils and injustices that Christ died to defeat continue to operate, wreaking havoc like Cain in the lives of the weak and innocent.

ANONYMOUS POWERS

In Ephesians 6:12, the apostle Paul wrote that "our struggle is not against flesh and blood, but against the rulers, against the authorities, against the powers of this dark world and against the spiritual forces of evil in the heavenly realms." Don't miss his implication here: The powers are more than pleased to hide under our human radar.

In the verse prior, Paul wrote, "Put on the full armor of God, so that you can take your stand against the *devil's schemes*." The greatest scheme of the devil is to have us believe there's no devil. As C. S. Lewis wrote in *The Screwtape Letters*,

> There are two equal and opposite errors into which [humans] can fall about the devils. One is to disbelieve in their existence. The other is to believe, and to feel an excessive and unhealthy interest in them. [The devils] themselves are equally pleased by both errors.[6]

The biggest scheme is having us believe that our battle is against flesh and blood. Said another way, the Evil One's great scheme is to convince us that the root problem is not with the Evil One but exclusively with ourselves, our circumstances, or our neighbors.

HOW DO THE POWERS
SEPARATE US FROM LOVE?

The powers and principalities throughout history have been oriented around many aims, one of them being to separate us from love. Paul alluded to this in Romans 8:38–39, when he named "powers" as one of multiple spiritual influences that can seek to separate us from the love of God.

One of their characteristics in their rebellious state is to separate us from love—love of God and love for each other through deception, division, and depersonalization. Why? Because love must be grounded in reality, nurtured in unity, and protected through the compassionate valuing of a person's worth and dignity.

- *Deception*
- *Division*
- *Depersonalization*

These three words serve as the (fallen) job description of the powers. Let's look at each word and, as we do, take inventory of our own lives. We are not untouched by these realities. As we consider each, let's ask ourselves, *Is there something here that is fragmenting my life or my relationships? To what must I pay attention to draw closer to Christ?*

Deception

In their fallen state, the powers and principalities of the world are fueled by lies. It's what sustains their presence in human institutions and societies. That failure to be true is also what separates us from love. Satan is named "the father of lies" by Jesus (John 8:44), and deception is the core strategy of the powers. It sometimes seems to be everywhere.

In both religious and nonreligious circles, lying is one of the most recognizable sins and seen as a serious character defect. From childhood, we hold truth telling as a virtue and rightfully correct our children when they are dishonest. Of course, the danger of lying is that if we do it enough, we begin to believe our falsehoods. We find ourselves creating a reality inconsistent with the truth and trying to inhabit it. Given enough time, we will eventually become our lie.

Yes, there's much work to do in this area as we form integrity, but sometimes it's easier to focus on *our* lies and overlook a larger culture of deception. In fact, the powers would love to keep us focused on our personal relationship with the truth and not have us look deeper into their deceptive ways.

We must take responsibility for the lies we tell and the deception we exhibit.

We must also recognize that we are acted upon by the powers in such a way that deception is rewarded and becomes a necessary means of survival.

The powers have one aim: to survive. They will do anything to have us feed their cosmic bellies, most prominently through deception. But the way the powers seek to have us live deceptive lives is not through explicit training in falseness but in convincing us to orient our lives around certain values (often good values, at least in the beginning) until they dominate us to such a degree that we can achieve them only through deceit.

For example, values such as productivity, efficiency, and performance are good values. There is nothing wrong with them. In fact, quite the opposite. But if they are allowed to bloat, if they are fed so much that they grow beyond healthy boundaries, they can become so overemphasized that it becomes impossible to live them out without resorting to deception.

Here's how that looked during one memorable moment in American life. In the late 1990s, Major League Baseball enjoyed a huge level of popularity. Prominent players like Mark McGwire, Sammy Sosa, and Barry Bonds were hitting home runs with such power and regularity that each game became a national spectacle. Major League Baseball was enjoying huge economic success and cultural attention. But that wasn't the whole story. In fact, these key players were performing at such a historic level—except with a little "help." Eventually, the truth came out: They were taking performance-enhancing drugs. The "story" of MLB was being sustained and even grown by cheating. There was no other word for it. Players taking illegal steroids won. Players who played fairly lost. And MLB had turned a blind eye to this shady practice—not just as a collection of individual players, coaches, trainers, or managers, but as a system that was larger than these individuals and had taken on a life of its own.

In the *Marquette Sports Law Review,* sports-law analyst Eldon Ham captured the big systemic lie in a report titled "The Immaculate Deception":

> Baseball is our oldest, most revered, most cele-brated major team sport, *but it let America down not just with steroids, but with deception.* Baseball looked the other way, perhaps hoping the steroid era would be without notice or blame, something like an "immaculate" deception. . . . But why the

arrogance? How did baseball believe it could get
away with such a ruse?[7]

In the case of Major League Baseball, the values of efficiency, productivity, and performance—translated into
greed—possessed a respected and trusted institution, creating a culture of deception that sought to grow, even at the
expense of that institution's true identity.

Division

By naming division as one of the strategies of the powers, I
mean to say that their intention is to have us participate in
what pastor and theologian David Fitch called the "enemy-
making machine."[8] The world we live in has, sadly, special-
ized in this.

Much of our society holds the conviction that if two
people disagree on important issues, they must be enemies.
Media, politics, and a host of other popular and powerful
opinion-making forces benefit from this conflict-based ar-
rangement. For far too many, disagreement is not *ever*
merely disagreement. It's deeper than that. Can't agree on
mask wearing in a pandemic? You're an enemy. Voted differently? You're an enemy. Different theological beliefs?
Enemy. On and on it goes.

The tendency to see people as objects to avoid or attack
because of our differences is a testament to our immaturity.
And when we fall prey to it, we are playing into the powers'
hands.

Depersonalization

Another strategy of the fallen powers is to form us to see
generic groups of people rather than individuals. If the

powers can have us relate to (and even hate, mock, or dismiss) categories of people instead of individuals—whom we all must acknowledge possess unique stories, pains, and gifts—it makes it easier to forget the humanity of those different from or disagreeing with us. Depersonalization is an act of desacralization. When we depersonalize, we stop seeing individuals as sacred creations of God. We begin to see them as an "it." When we are shaped to generalize unique, unrepeatable individuals, it makes it easier to keep them at arm's length or treat them with hostile force.

Doing this is the practical core of much bias and injustice. For example, if Black people can be lumped into one big category, it makes it easier for them to suffer through wrongful police engagement. If Mexicans can be consolidated into one big classification of murderers and rapists, it makes it justifiable to treat "them" with less dignity. If Palestinians can all be lumped as terrorists, it makes it permissible to bomb them relentlessly. If LGBTQIA+ people can be easily combined into one monolithic group, it makes for easy othering and discrimination. The list goes on. Whether we are talking about Conservatives, Liberals, Asians, or Whites, the great temptation is to see not people but socially constructed amalgamations of entire people groups.

Depersonalization is a weapon of the powers because if we can avoid the nuances of an individual's journey, we can comfortably refrain from relating to that person in a way that requires careful discernment. (Perhaps think back to the nice Southern mom at the beginning of this chapter. For her community to turn a young man's murder into a social event surely required them to practically cease to think of him as a person.) In my church, the matter of depersonalization is something we've had to regularly address as a congregation.

For example, since our inception as a congregation in 1987, New Life Fellowship has held the historic, traditional view of human sexuality as it relates to marriage. However, we have worked hard to hold this position with nuance and much grace. Sadly, we have failed from time to time, but we have also worked to learn, grow, and remain open and loving. This gracious approach was tested a few years ago in a particularly nuanced pastoral situation.

We found ourselves navigating a delicate matter. There was a married couple volunteering in one of our ministries. They were new Christians and loved the hospitality and grace they heard preached at New Life. They also were gay. When they began volunteering, they didn't disclose their marital status. It surfaced a few months later.

Many had come to love these two people, and they found community among us. When the news about their marriage was circulated among the pastoral staff, the approach taken was one of prayerful discernment. While we held to a particular theological position, we also recognized the unique story they carried. Honest conversations were had, and as a result, we didn't ask them to step down from their roles in ministry. It was a fragile moment, requiring unanxious, prayerful discernment. The issue was not our theological conviction but rather our expression of our commitment to see them as treasured and loved members of our community. (Several months later, the couple chose to step down of their own volition to seek a community that theologically affirmed their marriage.)

This community matter is one of the most challenging

scenarios within a church, and plenty will disagree on Conservative and Liberal sides, but in seeing the couple as precious siblings and image bearers of God, we were doing our best to resist the strategy of the powers to depersonalize. Depersonalizing at that moment would have led to immediate judgment and the subsequent removal from ministry. Zero nuance. Even less love.

Deception. Division. Depersonalization. All forces that fracture our world.

Think for a moment of your own life. How have you been possessed by the powers and their values of deception, division, and depersonalization?

THE CHURCH AS A POWER

At this point, a word must be said about the church and the ways it can become a possessed power. In his book *Moral Man and Immoral Society,*[9] twentieth-century American theologian Reinhold Niebuhr described the downward ethical spiral that often happens when we gather in groups as opposed to when we are alone. Generally, when we are alone, our morality is higher than when we gather with others. We see this principle at work in gangs, at political conventions, and on middle school playgrounds. We also see it with the church.

The church, since its inception, has lived with a dual identity. It has done wonderful things: establishing hospitals, serving the poor, working to abolish slavery, and inspiring people to live into a transcendent reality. These efforts have been both the work of individuals and the work of institutions. But at the same time—sometimes even in the same actions—the church has led violent crusades, embraced racism, perpetuated abuse, and aligned herself in compromising manners with political powers severely damaging Christian witness. We must understand and acknowledge this reality or we run the risk of rationalizing or becoming blind to our own shortcomings or even sin.

How, then, do we respond to all this? To begin, with awareness. One of the daily tasks of Christians and church leaders, denominations, and dioceses is to ask if and how we are being used by the powers and consider how we might better overcome them in the name of Jesus. We were not made for bondage to any force besides the love of Christ.

And so, after we routinely ask hard questions to raise our awareness—questions such as *What or who am I really serving with my time, belief, money, passion, and opinion?*—we must prepare ourselves to take real, peaceable, and decisive action to resist and conquer those powers, following the example of Jesus Christ.

UPROOTING THE POWERS

It's interesting how the standard application of the armor of God in Ephesians 6 has been so individualized that it plays right into the powers' hands. But Paul's words are collective encouragement for the forces at work:

> Put on the full armor of God, so that when the day of evil comes, you may be able to stand your ground, and after you have done everything, to stand. Stand firm then, with the belt of truth buckled around your waist, with the breastplate

of righteousness in place, and with your feet fitted with the readiness that comes from the gospel
of peace. In addition to all this, take up the shield
of faith, with which you can extinguish all the
flaming arrows of the evil one. Take the helmet of
salvation and the sword of the Spirit, which is the
word of God. (verses 13–17)

Truth. Righteousness. Peace. Faith. Salvation. The Word
of God.

Truth

When Dr. Martin Luther King, Jr., examined the world, he
articulated its fragmentation by naming the "triple evils of
racism, economic exploitation, and militarism."[10] In naming these powers with specificity, he exposed their strategies
by speaking the truth about them.

In my work in spiritual formation, I have preached on
the importance of naming things accurately. This is a significant part of truth telling. I have emphasized the need to
name interior messages that undermine our spiritual and
emotional health. But we must recognize that this is not
only an individual need and pursuit. We also need to examine the larger movements and structures of our communities and society.

Whenever we name the powers, we pull back the curtain
to see what's really going on. In this way, naming is apoca-
lyptic. It's a revelatory act. It's also liberating. I think about
this when engaging the power of technology. Author Sherry
Turkle, a professor at MIT, astutely argued, "We have to
love technology enough to describe it accurately. And we

have to love ourselves enough to confront technology's true effects on us."[11]

When our daughter started seventh grade, we purchased a mobile phone for her. For months ahead of time, Rosie and I discussed whether we should make this purchase. We knew that this new device would open our daughter up to a world she knew nothing of. It frightened us.

As part of our discernment, we researched a contract for our daughter to agree to, with all kinds of stipulations in it. We sat on the living room sofa and slowly read every line. Our goal as parents was not to ruthlessly control her but to name the truth and try to practically engage it, because the truth is that a phone's technology is more than a little computer processor, a screen, and a data connection. That's just what you hold. What it really is, is something that can be vastly spiritual— something with tremendous potential to shape a soul.

As her parents, we know that in the culture that our daughter finds herself in, there are spiritual forces that want to use that little hunk of glass and wires to form her in the way of deception (through highly edited photos), division (through hurtful gossip), and depersonalization (through the refusal to see people beyond their digital persona or avatar). As we went line by line through the contract, I began to see how I needed this talk for me as well! I too easily can be seduced by the possessed powers. We all can become blind to areas of spiritual bondage—and used to it.

Righteousness
If deception, division, and depersonalization are hallmarks of the powers, righteousness (often looking like truth telling, unity, and affirming the sacredness of each person) is

one of the redemptive strategies of God. In Isaiah 59:17, he is described as a warrior:

> He put on righteousness as his breastplate,
>   and the helmet of salvation on his head.

For Paul, righteousness—or justice—is one of the defining characteristics of those who are in Christ, and a powerful means to resist the powers. The powers thrive when the emphasis of faith solely focuses on private sinful behavior and self-oriented spiritual practices. They love when Christians turn a blind eye to poverty, abuse, and war without engaging the larger forces at work.

Going back to C. S. Lewis's *Screwtape Letters*—a book about a senior devil (Screwtape) instructing his nephew devil (Wormwood) in the art of temptation—I imagine what Screwtape might say regarding this kind of righteousness. Perhaps the old demon might write something like this:

> My dear Wormwood,
>   One of the most important tactics for keeping injustice present is convincing the humans that racism or classism is strictly an individual feeling of superiority. Don't let them focus on the institutional elements of it. Keep up the good work.
>
> Your uncle,
> Screwtape

Practicing righteousness in the daily small ways that show we are not in bondage to the lies of the world and instead are living free is vital for us as followers of Christ. As we work for justice, no matter how large or small our influence feels, the powers are pushed back in his name.

Peace

The powers and principalities are often fueled by violence and are willing to resort to it to expand and protect their reach. Paul responded to this by admonishing Christians to have their "feet fitted with the readiness that comes from the gospel of peace" (Ephesians 6:15). The peace Paul spoke of is not only the interior, spiritual, and psychological peace made possible through the Spirit, but the commitment to carry the good news of peace (wholeness, shalom) in a world of fragmentation. We resist the powers by choosing peaceful, nonviolent resistance to their dominion—a peace that is active, not merely passive. When we are asked to hurry, we should slow ourselves. When we are asked to forget others' humanity—especially if we disagree with them—we work to remember it twice as hard. When they tempt us to greed, we strive to be doubly generous. When they ask us to numb ourselves with mindless entertainment, we seek to cultivate the humble, attentive, rich life of the mind. We withstand their influence by becoming an unanxious presence in a world marked by anxiety. We withstand their influence by becoming daily more like Jesus, who lived without sin in the shadow of their false dominion and conquered them through the Cross.

We can uproot the powers by being peacemakers in our homes, schools, workplaces, cities, and world. In an increasingly divided world, followers of Jesus are to participate in making peace, not in making matters worse.

Faith

The shield of faith is the next piece of armor Paul detailed. The powers are best resisted when we trust in the One who fights for us. We overcome the powers not through trust in our abilities but through confidence in God's power. This is why prayer is such a powerful response to the powers. When we pray—alone or in community—we avail ourselves of God's empowerment to live in the way of Jesus. By faith, we open space for the Spirit to form our lives. By faith, we set our eyes on the One who will set all things right. By faith, we anticipate a world filled with the glory of God.

But faith is not something self-oriented. We are saved by faith, yes, but it's an outward-oriented faith. As the late theologian Marva Dawn noted, "The shield of faith signifies not only trust or confidence in God's power as a critical part of the armor, but also putting on the shield is to participate in Messianic faithfulness."[12]

Our faith is in the faithfulness of Jesus.

Salvation

The helmet of salvation should include liberation for others. We resist the powers not just by leading people to individually renounce them but by announcing salvation that extends to the larger social, economic, and political spheres of life that imprison people. Let me emphasize this point with a poignant observation from South African professor and bishop Peter Storey, who perceptively wrote,

> American preachers have a task more difficult, perhaps, than those faced by us under South Africa's apartheid, or Christians under Communism. We had obvious evils to engage; you have

to unwrap your culture from years of red, white
and blue myth. . . . You have to help good people
see how they have let their institutions do their
sinning for them.[13]

In the announcement of the gospel, we are called to
apply its power beyond privatized experiences of faith.
While holding on to the individual fruits of salvation, the
larger social and cosmic realities must be proclaimed and
worked for as well. Christ's death does not just apply to
"me." It must apply to "us."

The Word of God

Paul offered the sword of the Spirit as the final piece of
armor for the people of God. The sword, Paul noted, is the
Word of God. When most people read this, they automatically assume he's referring to Holy Scripture. In one sense,
this is correct. However, the Bible as we have it today
wouldn't be finalized until a few centuries after Paul's letter
to the Ephesians. It couldn't mean exactly what we mean by
it today. But, nevertheless, God's Word is critical for our
formation against the powers.

Here the Word of God is about two things: a life oriented by the careful integration of God's truth, and the
victory already established in Jesus.

Regarding the first way to understand the Word of God,
look at Jesus in the face of Satan's temptations. He consistently overcame demonic forces through the wise internal-
ization of Scripture.

When Jesus was tempted, Scripture flowed from his lips.
When he was challenged, Scripture flowed from his lips.
When he was crucified, Scripture flowed from his lips. One

of the ways to live like Jesus is to internalize Scripture so that when we are cut, it spills out.

Additionally, the Word of God is God's means of victory over the powers through Jesus Christ. Jesus is the Word of God, who has conquered the powers. This is the point I want to end this chapter on.

RADICAL VICTORY

When you read the Bible, you begin to see that the core issue is not whether we defeat the powers; that has already been settled. The gospel says that Christ is victorious over *everything*, including the possessed powers.

All through Jesus's life, he was disarming the powers. Every time he compassionately placed his hand on a marginalized person, he was revolting against powerful, spiritual messaging that declared that some people in society were contaminated and unworthy of touch. Every time he welcomed a sinner as worthy of love and belonging, he was rebelling against the powers that neatly divide the world into "us" and "them" categories. Every time he showed solidarity with the poor, he was rising up against the powers of greed. Every time he loved a religious outsider, he was overthrowing the power of religiosity.

Taking it further, when Jesus died on the cross, he didn't die just to forgive us of our sins. He died to destroy the work of Satan and disarm the powers. And the powers *are* defeated, though it still *looks* as if they are victorious in the world. This is the remarkable mystery of the Cross. In the Crucifixion, Jesus looks like a tragic failure, but he is the victorious one. He's victorious because in the kingdom of

God, the powers are not conquered by our mirroring them but by our resisting them. Jesus doesn't resort to the tactics of the powers.

On the cross, Jesus fully enacted what he taught throughout his ministry—namely, that the evil powers of our day are not defeated by doing what they do. They are defeated through suffering love. It's a strategy that works against the powers.

Let me explain it this way. I remember watching the blockbuster Marvel film *Black Panther* when it came out in the theaters. Without giving too much away (no spoilers!), the superhero suit that King T'Challa wears is made of vibranium. In the Marvel Universe, vibranium is the strongest substance in the world. It can absorb all kinds of energy that comes its way and redistribute it outward. Whenever enemies of the Black Panther struck him, he would store that energy and use it against them.

As I sat in the theater watching this story unfold for the first time, I thought about the Cross. Jesus obviously didn't have a vibranium suit, but he had in him the strongest substance known to the universe: *sacrificial love*. Jesus was able to absorb violence and cruelty: the lashes that tore his body, the nails that pinned his hands to the rough wood. He was able to absorb the crown of thorns on his head and the incredible pain and outrage of undeserved mockery and derision. What the powers could not see, however, was that he would redistribute a different kind of power that would defeat the powers of death through the very same things that they thought were defeating him. The powers are not defeated with the weapons of the world. The powers are defeated through the sacrificial love of God. That was true on the cross. It is true for us.

To say that Christ has disarmed the powers is not to na-ïvely suggest that we who are his followers are not often under their grip. But in Christ, we in fact *are* saved, *are being* saved, and *will be* saved from their dominion. We often think that if we can just organize enough, tweet enough, protest enough, vote the right people into office, then we will change the destructive ways of our culture.

The powers of the world are too strong to be overcome by us alone. Whether you're trying to triumph over a personal struggle or address societal problems, the powers are too strong to be conquered apart from God.

The world's problems are ultimately solved not through our action but through Christ's love. That's where we place our hope: not in something we do, but in something God has already done.

For now, the powers remain active, just as sin is a fragmenting reality for us all. Their mark can be seen on our lives and institutions. They are the spiritual forces responsible for much of the fracturing of our society. Consequently, you and I live as wound*ed* people and as wound*ing* people. Therefore, any treatment of the fractured world we see and feel must address the trauma we all carry. That's our next stop on the journey as we consider how we, like Christ, can become good, beautiful, and kind.

CHAPTER 3

HINDERING WOUNDS, HOLY WOUNDS

Trauma and the Hope of the World

We all know what it means to hurt. A world marked by *incurvatus in se* and the possessed powers wounds us. In the process of this outworking of sin, the way of love is uprooted from our lives, as is goodness, beauty, and kindness. Our woundedness or trauma has a way of hindering us from freely receiving and giving love. The pain we endure through experiences of betrayal, abandonment, and harsh words constrains us. The playfulness and openness we were created for become transformed into apprehension and suspicion. Our childlikeness is replaced with cynicism. Our experience of trauma has the potential to hinder our experience of love.

When I consider some of my own trauma, several memories immediately surface. One comes to mind, related to sports.

For years, I avoided playing sports in September. Odd, right? Well, one chilly September afternoon when I was a young man, I joined some friends and family members in a

game of two-hand touch football. In my Brooklyn neighborhood, the nearest park didn't have any grass—just asphalt. We played a very competitive game for a couple of
hours. As the game ended, I saw my opportunity and went
deep to catch a pass. I ran with everything I had and lunged
forward, closer, closer, almost making it. The whole world
slowed down as I felt the ball graze the tips of my fingers.

But there was a problem: An incredibly fast friend on the
other team had the same idea. We were both stretched out
for the ball when we collided. The impact awkwardly
slammed me to the ground. Trying to get back up and play
didn't work so well. The fractures and disjointed bones of
my right wrist were gruesome to look at. My play ended as
my father rushed me to the nearest hospital. I was in a cast
for a few months.

One year later, I found myself at the same park, this time
on the basketball court. I aggressively dribbled the ball,
gaining ground, driving hard. I was just looking to score,
when someone tripped me from behind. For a second time,
I hit that asphalt hard. *Not again.* I looked at my right wrist.
Mangled. Again. My father once again rushed me to the
nearest hospital to have my wrist put back into place. I was
in a cast, again, for months.

After those two painful moments, it took me years before I stepped foot on a basketball court or football field in
the month of September. It just felt wrong. What had been
so fun was now uncomfortable and ominous. Part of my
refusal was a sense of bad luck, but more than that, it was
trauma. My experience hindered the free-spirited love I had
for playing.

Those wounds have marked me in ways my mind has still
not fully processed.

But when put in perspective, my trips to the hospital are, at least for me, on the lower end of the trauma spectrum. Beyond the physical traumas our bodies experience, there are a myriad of mental traumas that wound us, and the common denominator is that they impede our call to love freely, generously.

EXPLORING OUR WOUNDS

If loving well is the essence of following Jesus, it requires the patient exploration of the stories beneath us, particularly the stories of our traumas and woundedness. To varying degrees, we are all carrying some level of pain, stored in our bodies and psyches.

In Bessel van der Kolk's seminal book *The Body Keeps the Score,* he noted that "one in five Americans was sexually molested as a child; . . . and one in three couples engages in physical violence. . . . A quarter of us grew up with alcoholic relatives, and one out of eight witnessed their mother being beaten or hit."[1]

In 2020, Barna Group, one of the leading market-research firms, published a study on trauma in America. Their research discovered that

> two-fifths of practicing Christians (40%) say their trauma was incited by the death of a loved one, the most common cause among this group. The next most mentioned cause of trauma was betrayal by a trusted individual, noted by one-third of the group (33%). Forms of abuse such as domestic violence (21%) follow in frequency.[2]

What is certain is that we are surrounded by pain from the past and are very likely carrying it in the present. Untended, the wounds we bear can lead to anxious reactivity and an inability to be truly "here," which often results in diverse attempts at suppressing our pain through escapism or the creation of alternate interpretations that we choose to believe instead of our own. Yet to be marked by love calls for a difficult but liberating discovery: It's in the compassionate confrontation of our wounds and trauma that we stumble toward wholeness, which, in turn, allows us to become agents of healing.

We often find it difficult to love well because we haven't understood the deep stories of trauma stored away within ourselves and others. This connection may seem a bit abstract, but it is real. When the trauma of the past holds us back from connection in the present (just like my two painful September injuries kept me from playing for some time), we encounter one of the invisible reasons that our world feels so fractured: We will always raise self-protective barriers in the presence of trauma. As a result, our ability to love well is severely compromised.

But there is a good invitation present here. Educator and author Parker Palmer has said, "The more we know about another's story, the harder it is to hate or harm that person."[3] Our exploration in this chapter is to produce compassion toward ourselves and empathy toward others, which are indispensable practices of love.

I recall having a conversation a few years ago with a congregant with whom I would regularly bump heads. I thought sometimes how we could not be much more different—theologically, culturally, politically, and generationally. I would find myself in tense conversations with him at least four times a year. Finally, there came a point when my pastoral sensitivity was waning thin. I felt done. I was ready to revert to my Brooklyn days—you know, angry scowls and choice words. As I drove down Queens Boulevard, preparing for yet another challenging conversation with this person, I noticed a call coming from another pastor on our staff.

"Rich, just wanted to check in. How are you?" asked the pastor. I responded with agitation, "I'm about to have another exhausting conversation with Harry."

"You know, Rich," said my wise friend, "Harry is the way he is for a reason. Do you know he experienced traumatic loss growing up?"

"Really?" I softly responded as I waited for the light to turn green.

"Really." And I began to hear more of Harry's story. How as a teenager, he'd been the one to discover the body of a dear, close family member who had died by suicide. How over the course of his life, other losses—significant, painful ones—had piled up.

After a long five seconds of silence (which felt like five minutes), I noticed the ever-present (in New York at least) sound of cars honking. Honking behind *me*. While I learned of Harry's devastating past, I forgot I was on the road. After anxiously hitting the gas pedal, I offered thanks to my team member. And though it would take some time to see it, in that moment on Queens Boulevard, something changed. My conversations with Harry were different from that point on. I've never seen Harry in the same light again. My grace for him had grown, even though no other circumstances in our relationship had changed.

To be sure, I didn't excuse or gloss over the moments

when Harry said or did something inappropriate, but something shifted in me. I began to see him as one longing for love but incapable of truly receiving and giving it.

The more we know about another's story, the harder it is to hate or harm that person—including ourselves.

THE LAYERS OF TRAUMA

Perhaps due to the stigma of mental illness, any notion of carrying trauma is often rejected by many in our communities, even including the church. But whether we want to acknowledge it or not, trauma is a distressing reality of life. It's more pervasive and present than we might think. Although people are remarkably resilient, the difficulties of life affect us.

There are many layers of trauma to be aware of, but let's start with a general view of it. The word *trauma* is a late-seventeenth-century word, Greek in origin, that literally means "wound." People who carry trauma have been somehow wounded, that much is certainly true. But let's go further.

Webster's dictionary defines trauma as "a disordered psychic or behavioral state resulting from severe mental or emotional stress or physical injury."[4] Author and therapist Resmaa Menakem described trauma as "a wordless story our body tells itself about what is safe and what is a threat."[5]

Draw those together: a wound, the state of woundedness, and the story that arises from living in that state. The world, rooted in *incurvatus in se* and possessed powers, is a state of constant wounding and re-wounding. These wounds range from the literal and physical to the emotional, social, psychological, and even spiritual.

Some of these wounds are fresh. Others are very old, even including *transgenerational trauma,* in which wounds of one generation affect subsequent generations in the same way that Menakem's "wordless story" begins a new chapter in a new life. Research has shown us in recent years that painful events get passed down to us even on an epigenetic, cellular level. We all have positive and negative legacies we must grapple with. As we say at our church, Jesus might live in your heart, but Grandpa lives in your bones.

Here's another example: Wounds that hinder love also come in the form of *racial trauma.* In her excellent book *Healing Racial Trauma,* Sheila Wise Rowe defined racial trauma as "the physical and psychological symptoms that people of color often experience after a stressful racist incident."[6] She went on to highlight the impact of racial trauma from a report that concluded, "The effects of racial trauma include fear, aggression, depression, anxiety, low self-image, shame, hypervigilance, pessimism, nightmares, difficulty concentrating, substance abuse, flashbacks, and relational dysfunction."[7] As a pastor in a very racially diverse city, I have had scores of conversations with people who have carried the weight of racial woundedness. It's a constant burden that far too many people must bear.

Of course, there's the wound of *sexual trauma* as well. The #MeToo and #ChurchToo movements are painful reminders that vulnerable people all over the world—in overt and covert ways—have not been treated as image bearers of God. This is another tragic example of structural and personal sin that must be denounced, lamented, and repented of, especially in the case of men who have bought into a cultural and theological narrative that sexual domination is our right. Much like racism, this narrative is deeply entrenched in the fabric of our society and requires a reimagined way to see and value women, made in the image of God.

Maybe you haven't experienced this level of overt woundedness. But before you skip this chapter, there's another layer that requires our attention, because the wounds we carry are not always observable. Some of the wounds we carry are developed over time and not relegated to a particular event. Much like fish don't know they're in water, people with developmental trauma carry it without realizing it.

In my first book, *The Deeply Formed Life,* I highlighted the nuances of trauma:

> When most people think of trauma, they think exclusively of catastrophic moments. But that is not the only way trauma works. Its presence often goes undetected, expressing itself in emotional distress that we consider to be normal. But make no mistake about it; to some degree or another, we carry experiences of trauma within.
>
> When I talk about trauma, I have in mind two sides of the same coin: getting what I didn't deserve, and not getting what I did deserve. In the first case, many people experience abuse (physical, sexual, or emotional) or undergo dreadful periods of loss. These are painful, psychologically scarring moments that can last a lifetime.
>
> In the second case, trauma is experienced due

to what psychiatrist Donald Winnicott refers to as "nothing happening when something might profitably have happened." In some homes, even though our parents or caregivers were always around, we never received the nurture, warmth, or attachment that we needed in order to flourish. Many families didn't know how to create environments in which we felt safe and seen. I find this to be a normal human experience. Each family has gaps, and sometimes those gaps unfortunately result in insidious ripple effects. When examining our families of origin, taking inventory of our trauma provides space for the Spirit to bring about healing. . . .

Regardless of the homes you and I grew up in, paying attention to the emotional system of our family is critical for our well-being and wholeness. Psychoanalyst and philosopher Robert Stolorow explained that developmental trauma occurs when "emotional pain cannot find a relational home in which it can be held." In other words, the pain we experience through everyday life has a way of metastasizing, damaging the rest of our emotional worlds.[8]

Further examination is needed around Winnicott's comment above. In his book *When the Body Says No,* Dr. Gabor Maté helped us with a clarifying question some of you might be holding: What about people who have not been abused or traumatized?

Maté, a medical doctor who has extensively studied the connection between stress and disease, noted that many people experience stress-related illness "not because something negative was inflicted on them but because something positive was withheld."[9] This is an important insight for all of us. Because human love will always be imperfect, we tend to carry gaps in our psychological, emotional, and relational development that must be tended to.

I remember preaching on the theme of exile one Sunday morning and being met by a congregant after the service.

"Pastor Rich," she said, "I've never seen my story explained in a church before like I heard it this morning. I just realized I'm in exile."

This immigrant from Pakistan was finally able to name the disorientation of being in a foreign land, with most of her family back in her country of origin. Her story is familiar in my part of the world, as half of the borough of Queens is foreign born. This international reality is clearly seen in neighborhoods like Jackson Heights. On one block, you can easily come across a Peruvian, Mexican, Korean, Dominican, and Chinese restaurant. What a gift. But beneath the glorious smells and tastes of the nations, there is loneliness, anxiety, and the constant existence of living "in between."

The pertinent question for our time, then, is what to do with it all. How do we live beyond our traumas? How do we witness to a power greater than our woundedness? How do we love in a traumatized world? That's what I want to focus on for the remainder of this chapter.

LEARNING TO LOVE IN A TRAUMATIZED WORLD

It can sometimes feel as if trauma is an ever-present reality among us. (It is interesting, isn't it, that Christ still bore the signs of his trauma in his body after the Resurrection?) In a sin-stained, broken world, trauma will continue to be with us. But, by the grace of God, it does not have to consume us. It can be redeemed. That is, for all its strangeness, the *good news* of the gospel.

But we are faced with two options: We can be wounded *wounders* or become wounded *healers*. Those in Christ—the true wounded healers—can join him in demonstrating the wholeness that love brings, whether individually, interpersonally, or institutionally. But it takes work.

The way to loving well in a traumatized world requires a level of compassionate self-confrontation deep enough to face ourselves, which in turn enables us to relate differently toward others. In short, the person we must learn to love is ourselves, primarily. It's very easy to focus on the traumas of others (and there's a place for that), but first we are called to open ourselves to the healing available in God's love.

Recognizing the ever-present reality of trauma is an important step toward the call to love well. In this recognition, we become aware of the forces that block the flow of love from our lives. In familiarizing ourselves with these blockages, we open ourselves to new possibilities that transcend our challenging and painful pasts.

Learning to love requires habits such as naming our shame, making sense of our stories, attending to our whole person (particularly our bodies), and beholding Jesus, our wounded, resurrected Lord.

Naming Our Shame

The first thing most of us must confess when trying to navigate our trauma is, *It's not my fault*. Traumatized people often carry great shame because they have been convinced that they are responsible for their wounds. This is almost never the case, particularly when the pain is the result of someone else's sin.

I've had many conversations with congregants who have been subjected to various kinds of serious abuse. Somehow in the process, they have internalized responsibility for the mistreatment. Women who have been abused by powerful men are often afraid to speak up due to fear and shame and feel that they are somehow to blame. Young adults reeling from years of sexual exploitation turn in on themselves, only deepening the wound. This is the agonizing and compounding reality of trauma. Not only do we carry the pain of the traumatizing moments, but we often bear the internal condemnation of shame as well.

When reading the opening story of the Bible, we see the two primary responses to sin on full display. When Adam and Eve take from the tree, shame and blame are the immediate results. In this story, *trauma* is not quite the best word to explain what happened there. I prefer other terms, like *rebellion, sin, pride,* and *underlying fear.* But shame is prominently featured as a primordial human reality.

Shame turns us in on ourselves, closing us off to others. It's impossible to be established in love when we are rooted in shame. Why? Because true love requires vulnerability. And as author and research professor Brené Brown eloquently noted, "Vulnerability is the greatest casualty of trauma."[10] This is an apt assessment of the human condition. Let me share a particular moment when this became clear in my own life.

Recently, I had a moment of interior breakthrough that surprised me. On a late weeknight, I was in my dining room reading resources on trauma. As I read stories of people naming their respective painful experiences, I began to examine my own history. I could not pinpoint a particular, acute moment of physical, sexual, or emotional abuse, but as I contemplated further, I began to jot down moments of woundedness and the beneath-the-surface impact it continued to have on my life.

When I was growing up, my family was very wealthy. Our wealth, however, was *not* measured in comfortably padded bank accounts, large homes, or expensive cars. In fact, we were quite poor as far as money was concerned. Our wealth was measured in joy, love, and warmth.

The truth is that there wasn't much money. That was often hard, and when it became visible, that lack of financial stability led to moments of shame. For several years in my childhood, our family was on public assistance to help make ends meet. Back in the day, government funds were not put on a debit card. Instead, we had to purchase groceries with food stamps.

One day (I must have been about twelve), I went to the bodega on the corner for eggs and bread. When it was time to pay, I took out our stamps and placed them on the counter. For whatever reason, the worker behind the counter looked at me and began to loudly point out to the handful of other people in the store that I wasn't paying with cash. He began making fun of my payment, and I heard snickers behind me. I was embarrassed. Ashamed.

From that point on, whenever I had to pay with food stamps, I made sure no customers were in the store, as I felt I could not bear further ridicule. I'd walk around the corner until the store emptied. When I saw that the coast was clear,

I'd grab the items as though I were in one of those *Supermarket Sweep* competitions. The messages I received from that one experience made me believe something was deeply wrong with me for being poor. That receiving assistance was something to be ashamed of, something even worthy of being mocked.

Fast-forward three decades. During the pandemic in 2020, the city of New York made a provision for all parents to receive four hundred dollars to pay for groceries. Due to the financial strain many families endured, the funds were to offset the financial pressure we all would be feeling. The four hundred dollars came in the form of a debit card, like what families on government assistance typically use.

Our family didn't *need* the extra funds, but we were grateful to have them. Soon after the card came, I went to the supermarket. When the cashier rang up my total, I took out the government-issued card to pay. As I did so, I noticed my hands shaking and my eyes averting the cashier's eyes. I swiped as fast as I could, grabbed my groceries, and speedily walked out of the supermarket. When I got into my car, I paused. Something had been touched deep within me. The dormant shame I felt in that bodega had boiled to the surface again.

Later that night, as I sat in my dining room, I named the feelings. I tried to reach for the deeper, subterranean messages stored away within me. I lifted my heart to God in prayer, listening. I filled pages in my journal with words of grace. I was able to name the various shame-scripts that had informed my relationship to money. In the silence, deep down I sensed God saying, *Rich, you are not your bank account. You are not your poverty or your financial wealth. You are beloved. You are treasured. You are mine.* In the naming of shame, I experienced a moment of breakthrough that continues to mark me.

Making Sense of Our Stories

As a pastor, I can often tell who is held in the grip of trauma. Usually, they are unable to tell their stories of brokenness with coherence. I'm constantly in contexts where I'm inviting people to share their story, name their wounds, and tell of the ongoing impact of that history. Some people—because of the interior work they've done—can name the moments of wounding that have affected them. For others, however, the task seems insurmountable. I've worked with incredibly articulate people who can speak eloquently on all kinds of topics yet don't have the verbal resources to talk about their woundedness.

Psychiatrist Curt Thompson highlighted the importance of parents making coherent sense of their stories. In his book *Anatomy of the Soul,* he wrote, "People who have made coherent sense of their own stories enable their children to attach [to them] securely. . . . In fact, of all the variables that influence the formation of a child's attachment pattern, *the single most robust factor is whether or not the parent has made sense of his or her own life.*"[11] Thompson's words are not just for those looking to be better parents but for all of us looking to be whole people. Making coherent sense of our stories is not simply about giving a chronological overview of our wounds. It's about being able to give expression to our story—especially the painful parts—in an unanxious, fully present, condemnation-free manner.

You see, whatever we cannot name reveals the insidious bondage we still exist in. Yet, through the love of God, we were made to live openly, at ease, and courageously, especially as we rehearse our woundedness. I'm talking not about flippancy but about a steadfast conviction that our wounds and trauma are not what identifies us. We are so much more.

To make sense of our stories requires us to gain some familiarity with them. In recent years, our culture has witnessed an enormous surge of interest in seeking to understand our stories and the connections we have to one another. Organizations that help trace one's genealogy and ancestry—even down to the geographical history of one's genes—have gained popularity due to the longing people have to understand their histories. However, the truth is that we can know all there is about our DNA but still not internally navigate our deepest interior stories. Yet we must do this if we are to live as healthy agents of change in the world, refusing to lie or ignore the truth about our journeys.

Facing the truth about ourselves and opening that part of our lives to God are imperative because God dwells only in reality. Telling our stories still proves to be enormously challenging. As Van der Kolk has written, "It takes enormous trust and courage to allow yourself to remember."[12] This act of remembering necessitates patient and healing spaces.

Community is one of our greatest resources when carrying trauma. There's no doubt that we can be (perhaps always will be) wounded in community, but for Christians, there is no escaping the truth that we are healed in community too. (Healing might not come from the community where the wounding took place, but community is usually needed for healing, nonetheless.) According to psychoanalyst Robert Stolorow, often trauma endures because "severe emotional pain cannot find a relational home."[13] Whether the community is found with trusted friends, a skilled therapist, or a healthy and prayerfully attentive group at church, we need relational homes where we and our wounds can be held.

Attending to Our Bodies

The acknowledgment of shame and the practice of making coherent sense of our stories are critically important for navigating trauma. However, moving toward healing requires something many of us are not used to: a deeper level of embodied engagement.

Theologian Shelly Rambo described trauma as a "living and intrusive reality."[14] Previous events intrude on us, sometimes without a moment's notice. When this happens, there is usually a physiological response. Our pulse might quicken. Our breathing gets shallower. We might notice our ability to think clearly is harder to access. Through responses like these, our bodies alert our minds that something painful in our psyches has been touched.

At New Life, we say, "Our bodies are major prophets, not minor ones." Our bodies contain knowledge that often takes our rational minds hours, days, weeks, or even months to decipher. This is one of the reasons attending to our bodies is so important. They are more than just "meat suits"; they are the holy and consecrated temples of God's Holy Spirit. While we still bear our scars, we must understand that God's will is that we find peace, righteousness, and well-being in our bodies. Although we must wait for the fullness of this, we can choose to move toward this reality now in Jesus's name.

HOLY WOUNDS?

Part of the reason that this holistic response is needed is because our Christian faith is incomprehensible without the ultimately redemptive trauma of the Cross.

The trauma of the Crucifixion is multilayered. Jesus experienced unspeakable physical trauma, torment, and a cruel, slow death. On other levels, he experienced rejection and mockery, relational abandonment, and the shame of being stripped naked in public, all culminating in the inconceivable trauma of mysteriously becoming "sin" for us (see 2 Corinthians 5:21), bearing the weight of God's judgment. In addition, the community of Jesus followers (including Mary, his own mother, who watched her son die) would be marked by unimaginable trauma in their own lives, through the agonizing witnessing of his brutal death. Yet, in all of this, God was at work. He was ushering in his kingdom, conquering the powers, and creating space for all of humanity to receive eternal life in his name.

The contemplation of Jesus as the traumatized yet risen Lord is important for anyone looking to understand trauma from a Christ-centered way. But our contemplation must take us beyond the Crucifixion to a particular encounter Jesus had with his disciples after the Resurrection.

TOUCHING THE WOUNDS OF JESUS

In John 20, Jesus's disciples locked themselves away for fear of being treated as Jesus was just a few days prior. In this moment of fear, they encountered the risen Lord (see verse 19). This wasn't the first time they encountered Jesus, but

Thomas, one of Jesus's disciples, had not seen the resurrected Jesus yet. Thomas had heard the testimony of his friends who excitedly shared the news of Jesus's surprising return, but Thomas needed more. He wanted to touch the wounds of Jesus himself. Well, Jesus provided him with that opportunity (see verses 24–29).

As they were gathered in a locked room, Jesus entered. He went to Thomas and invited him to touch his still-present wounds. The resurrected body of Jesus was somehow able to walk through walls and yet be physically touched. In this body, heaven and earth joined in unprecedented ways.

In her book *Resurrecting Wounds,* Shelly Rambo explored this story. She traced how prominent voices throughout the church have related to the wounds of Jesus and the connection such insights have in our often-wounding world. Among many questions here, one rises: If Jesus carries the scars from his traumatic crucifixion, do we carry our respective wounds into the age to come? Rambo explained that not everyone in the history of the church believed that the wounds Jesus carried were permanent. In particular, she singled out one of the most influential theologians of the Protestant Reformation: John Calvin.

In Calvin's commentary on the gospel of John, he taught that the wounds of Jesus were *temporarily* kept for the sake of accommodating to Thomas's lack of faith. In short, he showed his wounds to convince Thomas that it was indeed Jesus who was before him. The wounds, then, were not permanent but incidental—not a major part of the story. Rambo, however, argued that Jesus's wounds were more than just a minor detail.

I think she's right. And that matters.

In his wounds, Jesus shows himself to be one who identifies—even in a resurrected state—with humanity. Additionally, the wounds Jesus carries speak powerfully to his followers. We are all called to be wounded healers, but the first part of our healing requires us to be present to the wounds we have carried. In one especially notable quote, Rambo said, "The logic of 'wounds' in Christian thought is mixed. With wounds at its center, it has a curious history of erasing wounds."[15]

I find so much solace in the thought that the resurrected Jesus bore his old wounds—though surely redeemed—even on his risen body. Whatever it means for our future state, I believe that this has several lessons to teach us right now. First, it reminds me that our wounds don't have the last word. In Jesus's body, we simultaneously see broken humanity connected to but subjected to his glorious resurrected reality. One of the great promises of the New Testament is that this resurrection life is a reality that we can begin to live *now*.

In the wounds and trauma that mark our bodies and minds, those clinging to Jesus are given great hope that our wounds are not to be the controlling narratives of our lives. We are part of a larger, more beautiful story. Yes, we might have experienced great pain, but something greater than pain lies at the center of our existence: the healing grace of God's love.

Also, if Jesus carries his wounds on his body, we don't need to carry the shame of our trauma. As I mentioned earlier, there's often a great deal of shame that comes with experiences of trauma. But Jesus shamelessly retains the marks because they have been reconfigured into something miraculous, something indescribable. Imagine this being your story too. And yet it is—in Christ. Your wounds can be redemptively reconfigured. It's not that we have a sudden case of amnesia whereby we forget the traumas, but we remember in a different way.

In God's hands, our wounds become sources of healing, for ourselves and others. God wastes nothing, not even our deepest pain. Instead, the wounds that mark us are given a new narrative. No longer are we reduced to our worst memories. We now have access to imagine a new future. No longer are we subject to what happened. We now receive grace to show the world that something transformative happens when God's presence is invited into our stories. No longer do our wounds have to hinder love. In the grace of the Crucified One, we are given the resources to have our love deepened. In the language of Paul, we are crucified with Christ (see Galatians 2:20). We are united with the wounded Lord, and through this union, a new individual and collective life becomes available.

Finally, the wounds on Jesus's resurrected body serve as a much-needed reminder that each one of us have been or will be wounded in some way. This awareness is necessary to deepening our commitment to becoming a healing presence in this world. The world is a broken place. The wounds people carry are layered. Becoming whole requires a conscious commitment to becoming the healing presence of God in a wounded and wounding world.

To recognize that most people are carrying some form of woundedness is not to ignore or excuse patterns of improper (especially violent) behavior. It's unhealthy for us to soften our response to abuse.

We need wise boundaries. Naming the reality of trauma does not mean allowing the traumatized person to wound

other people in turn. On the contrary, it is to help us discern who we allow to lead us and who we place in positions
of power. When I became a pastor at New Life Fellowship,
part of my application process was to take an extensive psychological examination. The results would be shared with
the prospective leaders responsible for making the hire. Seeing that I was there to offer spiritual leadership to a very
large community, the wise leaders of New Life did their part
in creating wise boundaries.

There is obviously much more than can be said about
trauma and its effects on our lives. What's important to
hold on to as we close this chapter is the good news that
although our wounds remain, they can still be part of God's
redemptive purposes. Jesus knows what it means to be
wounded, and in him our wounds can become places of
deep connection with and compassion for others. In Christ,
our wounds no longer need to be marks of shame but can
become signs of grace. In God's loving embrace, we are no
longer hindered.

Making this happen takes more than intellectually as-
senting to this truth. It requires a new way of living, a reordering of our lives, a new set of practices. We must learn to
live, here and now, with the kind of connection, purpose,
and clarity that we all desire (and that God desires for us).
Amid fracturing relationships, fraying societies, and tempes-
tuous inner lives, we can and must find a way to live
wholly—to become daily a bit more good and beautiful and
kind.

Praise God, there is a way.

PART TWO

WALKING A BETTER WAY

CHAPTER 4

THE PROBLEM OF PRAYER

A Contemplative Path in a Thoughtless Age

The world is fractured in large part because of the quality of our prayers. Stay with me here, okay? The prayer that transforms the world is prayer that transforms us in Christ. Prayers exclusively oriented around what's happening *out there* (with them, in the world) mislead us into believing that the problem is rarely, if ever, *in here* (with us, in our inward selves).

To talk meaningfully about wholeness and love begins with a reappraisal of our prayer, because in so doing, we will be taking stock of what our souls deeply long for. Forming love is the ultimate goal of prayer. The power of prayer to heal the divides and transform the wounds of our world does not depend on its institutionalization ("If we only had prayer in schools again!"[1]). Our world is fractured not because there's no state-approved affirmation of "Christian" prayer but because many followers of Christ have not learned to pray in a way that opens us up to God's healing.

We see this multiple times a year in the United States after a mass shooting. After every such senseless and tragic

public murder in America, the world is painfully reminded
of, from one perspective, the impotence of prayer as various
public figures tepidly offer the cliché of "thoughts and
prayers" for the victims. After the Sandy Hook mass shooting, there were thoughts and prayers. After the mass shooting in Mother Emmanuel Church, more thoughts and
prayers. Parkland? Thoughts and prayers. Anti-Asian mass
shooting in Atlanta? Another round of thoughts and prayers.

As a culture, "prayer" has become code for a sentimen-
talism that is mildly sympathetic to tragedy but is helpless or
even apathetic to producing real transformation. The list
goes on, and I fear it will keep going on. The takeaway for
many of those who feel frightened, lost, angry, or grieving
is that such prayers are not doing what the world desperately needs.

In the face of tragedy, division, and hostility, not all
prayers are equal. Some lead to compassionate love: a force
with the power to turn a culture or redeem a life. Others
lead to a sentimentalized apathy that is the equivalent of a
spiritualized paralysis.

When most people think about setting the world right,
prayer is not usually at the top of their list of action steps. If
it is, it's usually presented in generic ways. This is because
our prayers have not done in us what we want to see done
in the world. Our inner lives are too often filled with un-
imaginative thoughts and disembodied prayers. Little wonder that nothing is done by them! But the way to address
this is not to give *up* on prayer but to give *ourselves* to prayer.
It is not to pray less; it is to pray differently.

Prayer is not about throwing holy words at God; it is
about embracing a new way of seeing. Prayer is not aspira-
tional fantasy; it is the opening of ourselves to the reality of

God's presence, an act that forms us in love. Prayer is meant to be where love is nurtured. It's in the true praying moment that God heightens our awareness that we are *already* enveloped in his loving union, which enables us to extend that love to others. We are shown the wealth of abundance that has always surrounded us in Christ. This path is the way out of *incurvatus in se;* it is resistance to the possessed powers and is the place God forms us to live beyond our wounds.

CONTEMPLATIVE PRAYER

There are many ways to pray. When I first became a Christian as a nineteen-year-old, I was given the A.C.T.S. prayer model (Adoration, Confession, Thanksgiving, Supplication). It's a good model. It gave me a helpful framework for praying. I even use it from time to time in group settings. I know many people who have utilized it as the way they seek to connect with God in prayer. But, ultimately, it hasn't been my *preferred* way to pray. I found myself frustrated and preoccupied with getting the model right and checking all the prayer boxes. Adore God? *Check.* Confessed my sin? *Check.* Gave thanks to God? *Check.* Offered prayers for others? *Check.* By the end of the prayer session, I would be either exhausted or a bit too pleased with myself for having checked all the boxes.

It was soon after my conversion to Christ that I was introduced to the Desert Fathers. The Desert tradition—first prominent in North Africa—began to surge two centuries after the resurrection of Jesus. It arose from a countercultural monastic community in the deserts of Egypt that was marked by practices of silence, solitude, fasting, introspection, and meditation. The communities that formed longed to follow Jesus in a way that cost them something. They were not content mirroring the decadence of the collapsing empire around them. They wanted to live in God for the sake of healing the world. This is why they fled to the silence of the desert—not because they preferred introversion but because they knew something powerful was available only in the contemplation that could come as a result of spiritual solitude, silence, and stillness. The same is true today.

Studying the way of the Desert gave me permission to be still and know that God is God (see Psalm 46:10). I would find that the way of the Desert moved me from needing a word from God to experiencing union with the Word of God. As I worked to grow in my ability to contemplate, not merely request in prayer, it became a sharing of hearts more than an offering of words. Certainly, words are an important part of prayer, but they began to flow from a different place, with the capacity to deeply change me, for the sake of love.

Before I define what I mean by this, it's important for you to know that anyone can do it. One doesn't have to be decades into a relationship with God to enter this kind of prayer. It is not for spiritual "experts" (whatever that would be) or for those holier than most. I have led my two young children in this kind of prayer and have trained adults well into their seventies and eighties at our church. Contemplative prayer is not for the spiritually elite but for anyone hungry for God. In truth, you can start right now.

As for a definition, here's a simple one I like to use: Contemplative prayer is the unhurried opening of oneself to God through silence, Scripture, and self-examination.

Let me briefly explain further. To contemplate something is to fix your attention on it in a curious and deliberate manner. Contemplation is what happens when you fall in love. It's what happens when you catch a beautiful sunset. It's what overtakes us when beholding an exquisite piece of art. We were made to contemplate. But here's the thing: Contemplation is not truly possible without a prolonged sense of attentiveness. Our pace must slow down. This is particularly difficult in a skimming and scrolling culture, hence the word *unhurried*.

In addition, contemplative prayer is not just about our pace but rather about space—in particular, our inner space. The person contemplating is not just a subject observing an object but a subject being encountered by another Subject (God). In this act of mutual beholding, the defenses we have built up come down slowly as we open our inner space to God's grace and love. That's what I mean by *opening oneself to God*.

The way to get there, I suggest, is primarily through silence, Scripture, and self-examination. As we gaze into the mystery of God's love in silence, unhurriedly listen to God's Word through Scripture, and attend to our own interior worlds, we position ourselves to live from a deeper center. As we give ourselves over to this way of being, we position ourselves to be changed—changed in a way that the interior fractures are gradually made whole.

BIBLICALLY GROUNDING CONTEMPLATIVE PRAYER

I've taught on contemplative prayer long enough that I know you're probably wondering, *Where is this in the Bible?* Well, I'm glad you asked. First, it's important to note that the Bible is not a systematic book with clear guidelines and instructions on all things related to faith and life. However, there are some important places in Scripture that will help us discern our way forward. In this section, I want to outline three biblical concepts that inform contemplative prayer. After we tackle this, we'll examine how this form of prayer roots us in love.

Biblical Idea #1:
God Is Closer to Us Than We Are to Ourselves

In Acts 17, the apostle Paul took a trip to Athens (see verse 15). This was a place known for its rich tradition of philosophical rigor. People gathered to debate and discuss the trending topics of the day. Consider verse 21, where it says, "All the Athenians and the foreigners who lived there spent their time doing nothing but talking about and listening to the latest ideas." Sounds like ancient Twitter and Facebook to me. As Paul toured the city, he found himself in conversation with the philosophers there. They could not understand Paul's gospel and asked for further explanation. In one section of Paul's presentation, he explained,

> From one man he made all the nations, that they should inhabit the whole earth; and he marked out their appointed times in history and the boundaries of their lands. God did this so that they would seek him and perhaps reach out for him and find him, though he is not far from any one of us. (Acts 17:26–27)

Then, in an act of missional brilliance, Paul attached his message to a famous quote by the philosopher Epimenides (verse 28):

"In him we live and move and have our being."
As some of your own poets have said, "We are his
offspring."

The words Paul offered serve as the biblical starting
point for contemplative prayer. First, God is not far from
any one of us. Second, in God, we live, move, and have our
being. Saint Augustine would pray in his *Confessions*, "You,
however, were deeper inside me than my deepest depths
and higher than my greatest heights."[2] Popularly translated,
"God is closer to me than I am to myself." This is indeed
one of the mysteries of faith. God is close, yet we are far.
God is inward, yet we live fixated on the outward. God is
present, but we remain absent.

Contemplative prayer begins here because it is a recognition that our prayers do not bring God to us but position us
to grow in awareness of God's nearness. In contemplative
prayer, we don't summon God but fix our hearts on the
truth that he is always summoning us to communion with
him.

Biblical Idea #2:
Christ's Work on the Cross Opens the Door
to Accessing the Presence of God

Christian contemplative prayer is a fruit of Christ's self-
giving love. In the book *Embracing Contemplation*, theology professor John Coe offered a biblical breakdown of
contemplative prayer. He wrote, "Christian contemplation
or contemplative prayer is grounded in an orthodox view of
original sin requiring the work of Christ in the new cove-
nant to reconcile humanity to God. Apart from this, the
human spirit cannot experience the Spirit of God (Eph

2:5)."[3] Said another way, communion with God is not some kind of human achievement but is always a gift from him—a gift most profoundly seen in Christ's work on the cross.

We see imagery of access in the temple on the day Jesus was crucified. There were different rooms, but the room you couldn't go into was called the Holy of Holies. What separated people from that room was a massive curtain. Only one person, the high priest, could go into that room, and only once a year (on the Day of Atonement).

The high priest had to be ritually and morally clean to enter this space. Legend has it that when the priest went in, there was a rope tied to his leg in the unfortunate event he needed to be dragged out of that most holy place.

When Jesus was crucified, he performed the dual roles of high priest and perfect sacrifice, and because of this, the curtain that separated people from the holy presence of God was torn in two (see Matthew 27:51). The curtain fell, resulting in the astonishing good news that people didn't have to tiptoe into God's presence. We could come boldly to the throne and presence of God. This is what the Cross secures for us. The Cross tore the curtain down so that we could meet with God. This is the foundation upon which Christian contemplation stands.

Biblical Idea #3:
We Are Invited to Dwell with and in God

Contemplative prayer is our yes to God's yes to us. It's one of the ways we seek to abide in Christ as he calls his followers to him (see John 15). If God's presence is available to us through Christ, the invitation is clear: We are called to find our home in God.

The idea of dwelling in God is one I think about daily—as

a matter of fact, every morning. I don't know when it started, but I became the tea-making person in our home. I don't drink much tea (coffee is my thing), but Rosie has it every morning. Making it for her is one of the ways I show my love for her. I have learned a few lessons over the years of my tea making. In particular, I've learned that there are at least two ways to make tea. Stay with me here. We're headed into deep waters.

The first way to make tea is to be a dipper. I'm a dipper. Whenever I enjoy a cup of tea, I dip the tea bag in and out, in and out. When the tea is to my liking, I self-approvingly wrap the tea bag around the spoon, press on the bag with the little tag, discard it, and enjoy the tea with my pinkie finger pointed out. For those taking notes, that's the first way to make tea.

But there's a second way. It's the way of the dweller. In this very sophisticated method of tea making, you place the tea bag into hot water and (wait for it) leave it alone! Although the transformation of water is slower, it's more potent. I remember having a conversation with a friend at a diner in Queens when this idea came up in conversation. He ordered tea. I had my coffee. I noticed he was a dipper too, although he didn't wrap the tea bag around the spoon. (Such an amateur.) I asked if he ever just let the tea bag steep in the water. He responded quickly, "Oh no, the tea will get too strong for my liking." I responded, "Well, that's a mighty metaphor."

He stared at me with his eyebrows up, waiting for me to expound on this revelation.

I would explain that the word *dwell* in the Amplified Bible version of John 15 comes from the Greek word *meno*. It's a term that comes up more than sixty times in the gospel of John. Over and over, the invitation from Jesus is to dwell, abide, remain, and stay with him. This is the essence of contemplative prayer. In contemplative prayer, our aim is not to do something for God, or even gain something from him; it's simply to *be* with God.

The three simple biblical ideas I just offered serve as a good foundation for contemplative prayer. At this point, I want to focus on the mystery of contemplative prayer and why we need it to resist the uprooting of love in our lives.

EVERYDAY MYSTICS

What our world is desperately searching for are people who are living from a depth of life saturated with God's presence of love. Karl Rahner, one of the foremost theologians in the twentieth century, famously said, "The Christian of the future will be a mystic or will not exist at all."[4] For Rahner, a mystic is not someone who gets some kind of secret spiritual knowledge; a mystic is someone who has a genuine experience of God. Many people are nervous about the word *mystical,* and with good reason. Mystical experiences can lead to manipulation, dissociation, and downright weirdness. But mysticism is far less a threat to our world than we think. It's a needed gift.

To commit yourself to contemplative prayer does not mean that you will be granted all kinds of visions and esoteric experiences. Surprisingly, experiences are not the goal with contemplative prayer. Those who live for experiences will find themselves relating to God as a cosmic vending machine, banging on the glass when the spiritual item they want is stuck beyond their reach. Contemplative prayer, however, is allowing your soul to be kissed by God in ways that go beyond what we can feel. What is a mystic, then? Simply someone who takes the radically available presence of God seriously.

This is important because transformation through contemplative prayer is not something we can effectively grasp, nor is it something we can thoroughly observe in a lab. Certainly, we can see the connections between contemplative prayer and our neurology (as I explore later in this chapter), but transformation is beyond our concrete understanding. The only thing we can say, in faith, is that God meets us. In fact, what matters most in all this is whether our lives are markedly different through contemplative prayer. *Am I being formed into love?* is the ultimate question worthy of investigation. In what follows, I'll demonstrate how this kind of prayer helps us face our "false self," how it forms us to be an unanxious presence, and, finally, how it empowers us to steward our words.

FACING OUR FALSE SELF

One of the great hindrances of love is found in our false self. If our true self is found "hidden with Christ in God" (Colossians 3:3), our false self is a constructed identity that in some way tries to play God. One of the ways this happens is by locating the problems of the world "out there." It is possible to pray in such a way that our false self is never confronted, which is why contemplative prayer is so needed.

In contemplative prayer, we entrust ourselves to God, giving the Holy Spirit space to reveal the inconsistencies within, the intense imaginary conversations stored in our minds, and sins we need forgiveness from—all important for loving well. It's hard to do so when the problems are always outside of ourselves. But until we give ourselves consistently to this work to confront our own demons, we will project them back out into the world and fail to see that some demons in the world are reflections of ourselves.

One of the reasons contemplative prayer is socially subversive is because in this kind of prayer, our personal contradictions are revealed. And when we can reject illusions of ourselves, we can live with greater discernment as we engage the world.

I often think about Jesus in the wilderness as he was confronted by the Evil One. After he was baptized, he was led into the desert by the Spirit (see Matthew 4:1). While there, he fasted and was tempted by Satan. Satan presented him with three seductive invitations to be a Messiah, formed by a self-serving appetite (turn this stone into bread), self-oriented performance (jump from the temple and angels will catch you), and self-obsessed power (bow and all the kingdoms will be yours). In the wilderness—which would be a very quiet place, conducive for contemplative prayer—Jesus's motivations were tested. What kind of Messiah would he be? One who lives from the center of his own needs and desires, or one marked by self-giving love? We know from the Gospels that Jesus chose the latter way of self-giving love.

I find it fascinating that this forty-day period was a significant part of Jesus's journey. On one level, he was reenacting the story of Israel but with a different outcome. Israel went through the waters of the Red Sea but failed repeatedly in the wilderness. Jesus went through the waters of baptism but succeeded in obedience to the Father in the wilderness.

On another level, however, Jesus, in the silence of the desert, was confronted with himself and, in the process, clung to the testimony of Scripture as well as the affirming word of the Father spoken at his baptism. This, I believe, is one of the by-products of contemplative prayer. In contemplative prayer, our impure motives, repressed anger, unprocessed pain, stubbornness, and lusts emerge. Part of this revelation is to lead us to repentance and humility. We need God to work on us.

One of the reasons I don't like contemplative prayer is because it gives God too much authority over my life. I say this tongue in cheek. There have been plenty of moments when God used this time to suggest an area of pride, apathy, or misplaced anger in my life.

For example, I recall receiving an email with words of gentle critique about a sermon I gave. The person felt hurt by my perceived indifference to a social issue that this person wanted me to address. I read the email with irritation and deleted it twenty seconds in. I moved on with my day, working on a sermon and making a few pastoral calls, and then as bedtime approached, I sat down for a time of contemplative prayer.

I set the timer on my phone to seven minutes, opened my hands toward heaven, took a deep breath, and two minutes into it, I was reminded of my quick decision to delete that email from that well-meaning congregant. I sensed God calling me to go to the recently deleted items in my email list, look at the message again, and offer a pastoral response the person rightly deserved. I can't tell you how many times the

Holy Spirit does this in me. It's when I open myself to God that he has the space to work in my soul.

As Jesus had to consider his life in the wilderness, I must reflect on mine in the city. *What kind of Christian am I?* One who lives according to my own appetite or self-obsessed power, or one who desires to be shaped by Jesus's self-giving love?

BEING AN UNANXIOUS PRESENCE

In 1987, I was eight years old. I vividly remember a commercial that contained one of the most culturally remembered images and phrases ever since. The commercial was called "This Is Your Brain on Drugs." In the fifteen-second version, with ominous music in the background, the commercial begins with butter or oil sizzling in a frying pan. A dull voice of a man says, "This is drugs." Half a second later, an egg is thrown into the pan, and the man adds, "This is your brain on drugs. Any questions?"[5] As an eight-year-old, I had lots of questions. But the point of this public service announcement was to give a powerful metaphor describing how fried our brains get through drug use.

We need another public service announcement for our day. We need a "This Is Your Brain on Silence" commercial. In recent years, there's been much research around the neurological impact silence and meditation has on our brains and, consequently, our lives. Contemplative prayer has been one of the ways we have discovered what Paul was getting at in Romans 12:2. He wrote, "Do not conform to the pattern of this world, but be transformed by the renewing of your mind." Most people interpret this verse to mean memorizing the Bible (a great practice), but that's just one way to renew our minds. We are learning that there is something powerful at work when we give ourselves to contemplative prayer and meditation.

In his book *How God Changes Your Brain,* American neuroscientist Andrew Newberg performed brain scans on Franciscan nuns, Buddhist practitioners, and Pentecostal believers to see how their brains reacted to prayer. I find these conclusions pertinent for this chapter:

> Intense, long-term contemplation of God and other spiritual values appears to permanently change the structure of those parts of the brain that control our moods, give rise to our conscious notions of self, and shape our sensory perceptions of the world. . . .
>
> Contemplative practices strengthen a specific neurological circuit that generates peacefulness, social awareness, and compassion for others.[6]

In short, the obvious conclusion seems to be that practicing contemplation can permanently and positively change our lives and our world. One of the chief benefits of contemplative prayer is the lowering of anxiety and anxious reactivity. I wonder if that is why we never see Jesus exhibiting anxious reactivity in the Scriptures.

Jesus spent much time in solitude and silence, and even with the unrelenting pressures around him, he never succumbed to them. Contemplative prayer forms us to love well because love requires calm presence over reactivity. In contemplation, our brains are rewired, giving our bodies the expanded capacity to be present with ourselves and others. Contemplative prayer forms love in us because it aids us in addressing our dark sides, renews our minds, and trains us to discern our words.

STEWARDING OUR WORDS

I remember the summer of 2001. I had been a Christian for two years. One morning, as I read through the book of Proverbs, I came across this verse: "In the multitude of words sin is not lacking, but he who restrains his lips is wise" (10:19, NKJV).

I was struck by these words and committed to restraining my lips. Well, it didn't last long. As a relatively new, zealous Christian, I was too fixated on correcting others (like the time I called a Christian TV program and berated a customer service representative because I detected heresy on the show), arguing with people who held different faiths (like the time I invited a group of Jehovah's Witnesses to intensely debate me in my Brooklyn apartment), and proudly demonstrating the newfound knowledge I'd gained an hour prior. I loved to talk. Still do. God help me.

Over the course of my journey in following Christ, I would learn that limiting my words was more than a matter of willpower. I needed God to work in me. The Desert Fathers would prove to be a guide for me in this area. Here are two of my favorite sayings of theirs:

> They said of Agatho that for three years he kept a stone in his mouth in order to teach himself silence.[7]

Abba Isidore of Pelusia said, "To live without speaking is better than to speak without living. For the former who lives rightly does good even by his silence, but the latter does no good even when he speaks."[8]

I recognize that as you read these, you're probably thinking how impossible this way of life is. But my point in highlighting these quotes is to help us live from a different place.

It is not a stretch to say that we live in the most overly communicated age in history. There's a lot of chatter in our world. The blessing in this is that essentially everyone has access and a platform to speak. The problem with this, as you know, is that everyone has access and a platform to speak.

Every second, on average, around 10,000 tweets are tweeted on Twitter, which amounts to 60,000 tweets sent per minute, more than 900 million tweets per day, and almost 300 billion tweets per year.[9]

That's a lot of talking and tweeting!

The problem with all this is that often our lives are not saturated with silence, which means our speaking often comes from a place not rooted in God. Instead of our words carrying power to expose the powers, announce the kingdom of God, and gently encourage those bruised by life, they too often resemble the words of the fallen world system. The question, then, is, What do we need? My answer is contemplative prayer; we need more silence; we need a life of being with God.

Contemplative prayer is not just a surrendering of words in silence before God. It's also the training of the soul for moments when we must surrender our words before others (especially when we are tempted to use our words for harm).

Circling back to the book of Proverbs, there are many themes within this popular book of the Bible. There are many themes within the thirty-one chapters, but Proverbs has more to say about our words than about anything else it addresses in our lives—more than money, sex, or family. The repeated calls to use our words wisely reminds us how much our words matter—in conversations, emails, texts, blogs, and phone calls and on social media. Much of the tension in our families and offices and dorms and churches and nations is because of undiscerning words.

Contemplative prayer trains us in self-control, kindness, and love, which are all part of the fruit of the Spirit. But how do we live this? For the rest of our time, I want to give some contemplative-prayer guidance. Again, it must be said that practicing this kind of prayer once or twice might not yield much fruit. It's in the sustained, regular repetition of it that God helps us learn how to love.

CONTEMPLATIVE PRAYER
FOR BEGINNERS AND EXPERTS

For those trying to establish a life of contemplative prayer, I laid out several guidelines in *The Deeply Formed Life*. I wrote about the importance of befriending silence, reframing distractions, and remembering that God is always waiting for us with open arms. For our purposes here, I want to get very practical and model how I practice contemplative prayer. The cool thing about contemplative prayer is that it works the same for beginners and experts. I've met with

Christian monks who have given decades of their lives to contemplative prayer and have led teenagers in this practice. It works the same no matter who is doing the praying.

When I sit down to pray in this way, I place my feet solidly on the floor. This reminds me that contemplative prayer is not to lift me out of this world but to help me remain connected to this world but from a different center. I settle in, take a few deep breaths, and open my palms as an expression of opening myself to God's presence and love.

I usually set my phone timer to a few minutes— sometimes five, ten, or twenty. For those new to this kind of prayer, it's perfectly normal to look at your phone to see how much time has passed. When I first started praying this way, I was sure I was praying for ten minutes. When I looked at my phone, only two minutes had elapsed! Don't worry— you'll get accustomed to it.

With my phone timer set, my feet planted to the ground, and my palms open, I usually have a word or phrase to keep me connected to God when I get distracted. I often simply say, "Jesus" or "Lord, here I am." I've also used words like *peace* and *Holy Spirit*. I softly whisper one of these terms while in prayer. There are times when I can't shake a particular distracting thought. It often has to do with an errand I need to run or idea I should explore. Sometimes it's an imaginary conversation with someone I'm at odds with. While I try to limit doing this, if I get too distracted, I pause to write down an important next step I need to take after my time of prayer.

After offering my heart and body to God in this way, the alarm goes off. From there, I'll slowly read an excerpt from one of the Gospels or meditate on a psalm or two, paying attention to what God might be saying to me. When something resonates, I often write out a prayer or reflection in my journal. Sometimes my journal entry is two sentences, sometimes two pages. After writing, I slowly pray the Lord's Prayer and close with another minute of silence. You will ultimately have to find your own way, but hopefully this serves as a start.

The challenge about contemplative prayer is that you rarely see fruit in the moment. It's often in retrospect that you see the impact of this practice, which is why we are called to persevere in it.

As the Quaker Douglas Steere has said, "Stopping too soon is the commonest dead-end street in prayer."[10] His statement should remind us that the point of this kind of prayer is not to measure the change we want to see but rather to meet with the God we do not see. It just so happens that meeting with God will bring about great change; we are just unaware of the depth of change within ourselves.

CHAPTER 5

BEYOND THE WALLS OF THE FALSE SELF

Humility and Lowering Our Defenses

One reason the world remains deeply fractured is that there's too much to defend. This is particularly true *within* us. The interior walls we build are too deep and too high to root us in love. Why do we have a hard time navigating conflict? Why do we find it excruciating to receive criticism? Why are we filled with anxiety over the disagreements we have? Perhaps it's because we have constructed a life that needs constant defending. It's something I'm familiar with.

I remember my first time preaching at New Life. Pete Scazzero, who was the senior pastor at the time, called me aside in the church lobby after I delivered my sermon. Just prior to our conversation, I was shaking hands with congregants and hearing delightful words of encouragement.

"Pastor Rich, thanks for that word," one had said. "God spoke right to my heart, pastor," said another. I was feeling pretty good about my twenty-eight-year-old self, when Pastor Pete called me to the side. Evidently, there was a post-service practice of reviewing the sermon. The goal was to help strengthen it for the following service. When he called me, I noticed he had a legal pad with all kinds of notes scribbled on it. I had a sense something was coming. I was on edge.

"Great sermon, Rich. Way to go," he said. "Do you know what you can do to strengthen it for the next service?" I defensively thought, *Do you know what you can do, bro?*

What was happening in me? In that moment, something was touched. My guard went up. My defensiveness was clear as day—to me at least. Pastor Pete would go on and give poignant tips for taking the sermon to the next level. I took down some notes but was still bothered. My lack of humility in this moment made it difficult to connect with him and see his feedback as a gift. You see, humility is not just doing a lowly task; it's a life committed to the hard task of lowering one's defenses.

When we envision humility, we often think about taking on menial duties no one else wants to do. And, of course, that's a facet of it. We have in mind someone who doesn't seek the spotlight but shines the light on others. Again, another good image of a humble life. But the angle of humility that we desperately need for our fractured world is seeing it as the ability to live freely from protecting the false self—living free from the defensiveness that closes us in on ourselves.

The fractured relationships we experience emerge out of our inability (or our refusal) to lower our defenses. Instead of seeing companions, we see competitors. People who disagree with us are viewed as threats to be eliminated. The walls we build are for one reason: to protect the false self.

REFUSING TO PROTECT THE FALSE SELF

The *false self* is a term many use to describe the identity we construct that conceals the true self found in Christ. It's an important term to consider in relation to humility. Consider three perspectives.

Thomas Merton has said,

> Every one of us is shadowed by an illusory person: a false self.
>
> This is the man I want myself to be but who cannot exist, because God does not know anything about him. And to be unknown of God is altogether too much privacy.
>
> My false and private self is the one who wants to exist outside the reach of God's will and God's love—outside of reality and outside of life.[1]

In his book *The Deeper Journey,* Robert Mulholland, Jr., said, "My false self, like most false selves, is a control freak that manipulates people and situations to protect it from disturbances to its status quo."[2]

And, finally, the Franciscan author Richard Rohr powerfully captured the agenda of the false self. He wrote, "The agenda of the false self is to look good, to pretend. . . . You can tell when the false self takes over because you become easily offended. The false self . . . is offended (about every three minutes) because it is fragile. The true self, on the other hand, is unoffendable."[3]

The true self is the place within us where we are found securely wrapped in God's love and have no need to project or protect it. The true self finds its identity in something much deeper than human words of approval or criticism. The false self is incapable of this level of freedom, but it is where most of the world lives from.

Humility, then, is the ongoing commitment to live from the true self. Not an easy task, I know.

SOUL FRAGILITY

I'm reminded of this difficulty on a regular basis as a pastor. While some might assume—because I'm a pastor—that I'm emotionally centered, eager to be present with others, and not easily affected by criticism, I know the truth (as does my wife) of my "soul fragility."

Soul fragility shows itself when you get an email from someone who wants to discuss an important matter and your interior walls go up five seconds into reading it. Soul fragility is present when a blind spot of yours is identified by a friend and you emotionally move away from that person as a result. Soul fragility happens when someone on social media disagrees with your post and you go ahead and mute or block them without even entertaining what they are saying. Every time our false self is threatened, it reveals the fragility we carry.

Humility is the antidote to soul fragility. Or said another way, fragility can be a doorway to humility. Our fragility is one of the most important signs that the false self is running the show. And when we allow ourselves to be led by our fragility instead of protecting it, we open ourselves to a way of life marked by internal freedom, no longer governed by the words and actions of others. This is what Jesus offers us in his most important sermon.

BLESSED ARE THE POOR IN SPIRIT

Jesus, the perfect personification of the humble life, calls us to live in the humble way of God's kingdom, a way marked by poverty of spirit. This way forms us toward wholeness. Poverty of spirit is language Jesus gives in the Sermon on the Mount to describe our utter dependence on God. Truly, our lives are found to be rich in him to the degree that we recognize our inner poverty. The poor in spirit are those who refuse to build a life apart from the love of God.

Poverty of spirit is living detached from the incessant need to cling to things that prop up our false self. In this regard, it's the gradual movement toward a nonreactive and carefree existence, living freely from the depths of God's acceptance.

The person who is poor in spirit doesn't live a self-protective life. For this person, there's nothing to *protect,* nothing to *possess,* and nothing to *prove.* Let me briefly comment on each of these words.

Nothing to Protect

When you are poor in spirit, there's nothing to protect. In other words, there's no need to live covering your weakness and failures. Most of life is lived concealing our deficiencies from others. We are trained to put our best foot forward. We are conditioned to make a good first, second, and third impression. Now, don't get me wrong—this is important. When you go on a job interview, it's only right to put your best foot forward. It becomes a problem only when all of life is about making a good impression.

The poor in spirit don't need to protect an idealized version of themselves. This is something the ancient Desert

Fathers and Mothers teach us. In the first few hundred years after Christ's first coming, men and women fled to the desert to commit their lives to prayer, silence, fasting, and the building of community. In these holy places, there was plenty of drama. I'm strangely relieved when I read of the conflicts and pettiness among this group of people. It's not just us who have a hard time living without conflicts. In one of the most popular sayings of the desert tradition, we have this:

> One of the old men who saw it became a prey to jealousy and said to him, "John, your vessel is full of poison." Abba John [the leader of this monastic community] said to him, "That is very true, Abba; and you have said that when you only see the outside, but if you were able to see the inside, too, what would you say then?"[4]

This is a person who is poor in spirit. Nothing to protect. I hope you see the freedom of this way of life. It's exhausting to live protecting and defending ourselves. The humble person recognizes that there are so many issues beneath our lives. The faster we can own this, the freer we can be and the more loving in the process.

Nothing to Possess

Those who are poor in spirit have nothing to possess. By this, I'm not saying that we don't own property or save for the future. Rather, I'm saying that the poor in spirit live radically detached.

To live with nothing to possess includes not counting on

the opinions of others in order to feel good about ourselves. Remember, the facet of humility that I'm trying to drive home is about letting go of the need to cling to a self we believe we must project out to the world. Why is this important? Well, in short, when we live according to a healthy detachment, we can be present with others. Our sense of well-being is not established through the praise or criticism of others. It's found in being claimed by God.

Nothing to Prove

To be poor in spirit is to live free from the need to prove or justify ourselves. Jesus calls these people blessed because our righteousness and belovedness transcends our limited attempts to make something of ourselves. Much of the in-terpersonal problems we encounter—whether in marriage, church community, or the workplace—stem from our need to prove ourselves, win an argument, or exercise power over another. But the humble live free from this. I'm reminded of a well-known story told of the Christian philosopher and acclaimed author Dallas Willard.

One day, Dallas was giving a lecture on a university cam-pus. During the lecture, a student brashly challenged the professor in front of the class. Author and speaker John Ortberg recounted the story:

> Toward the end of one of his philosophy classes a student raised an objection that was both insult-ing toward Dallas and clearly wrong. Instead of correcting him, Dallas gently said that this would be a good place to end the class for the day. After-ward, a friend approached Dallas: "Why did you

let him get away with that? Why didn't you demolish him?" Dallas replied, "I was practicing the
discipline of not having to have the last word."[5]

The discipline of not having the last word is humility in
a nutshell.

When Jesus offered these words at the beginning of his
most famous sermon, he was opening a portal into life in
the kingdom of God. The humble are those who live in the
fullness of this kingdom because they have nothing to
prove. Their lives are found in God's love. They have nothing to protect because they are not surprised by their own
inconsistencies and contradictions. They have nothing to
possess because they have been possessed by God's love,
which makes grasping and clinging unnecessary. It's such a
free life, unencumbered by the need to protect the idealized
version we put forth.

Imagine with me for a moment a world marked by this
kind of humility. Imagine your family and your church
being that way. Imagine you, being the kind of person who,
when approached by someone upset by something you said,
doesn't try to protect, possess, or prove anything. What if
you were free enough to say, "Tell me more about what you
see." Imagine you're about to head into a difficult conversation. What if you, by God's grace, decided to ask more
questions rather than give self-justifying responses? Imagine
going to bed at night not clinging to an idealized version of
yourself but resting in the gracious love of God. These are
very real possibilities for the world we live in—and not just
for our personal lives. God wants to empower us to live
humbly for the larger, viscerally polarizing issues we face.
How can the world be healed without humility?

The world needs individuals and communities who can live from a humble center. It's a place of wholeness; it's the location where love gets formed.

One of the greatest gifts we give the people we lead (and generally the people we are in relationship with) is a lack of defensiveness. One of the marks of a healthy culture and a healthy soul is the willingness to be curious, open, teachable, and humble.

As I think about Jesus heading to the cross, I realize there is no defensiveness in him. In the Crucifixion, his body, nailed to the wood, was an expression of his refusal to vindicate or defend himself. He left that up to God. For us to be crucified with Christ calls us to the same way of being. I'm not suggesting that we subject ourselves to abuse and mistreatment. I have in mind our willingness to lay down every identity we have constructed that we believe we need to defend. But wherever there is defensiveness in us, it reveals an area of our lives that is not crucified with Christ.

You might be wondering what this has to do with love. Everything.

Our lack of humility closes us off to the love of God and the gifts of needed insight from those around us. To lower our defenses is to make space for others and the gifts they carry. We see this in one of the great stories of the Bible.

DROPPING OUR ARMOR

One of the great biblical stories on humility comes from the life of Naaman (see 2 Kings 5). It took a great deal to get him to humbly submit to a way that ran contrary to his deeply entrenched self-importance, but he got there, nonetheless. In the process, he was physically, emotionally, and relationally restored.

Naaman was a highly regarded leader who commanded many in the Syrian army. I'm sure he would give inspirational speeches in this role. He would galvanize the troops, leading from a place of operational competence and strategic brilliance. He was all that and a bag of chips. But he had leprosy.

Leprosy was the Covid-19 of the day. It was a vicious skin disease that attacked the body, and the effects were horrendous. On many occasions, leprosy would cause fingers and toes to fall off. Limbs would be damaged. Leprosy resulted in a loss of sensation in nerve endings, as well as damage to more body parts. Some have said that the disease can take thirty years to run its course, and in that time span, entire limbs can simply fall off.

Beyond physical pain, however, I imagine there was deep psychological pain as well. We don't know much about how Naaman dealt with this, but it's evident that he must have lived hiding from others. He covered himself with his armor, but he knew the truth about himself.

The story goes on to say that Naaman had a servant, and she was from Israel. She must have seen the pain and agony Naaman experienced at home and wanted to help. In passing, she brought up a prophet from her hometown, named Elisha. She had a sense that this prophet could heal her boss. Naaman decided to pursue this recommendation.

After arriving in Israel, Naaman was given directions to Elisha's house. Naaman showed up with an entourage that would make some hip-hop artists envious. He went to see Elisha with horses and chariots. After a long journey, he knocked on the door. No answer. He knocked again. Elisha knew he was coming, but still no answer. Another knock. Finally, the door opened. At the door stood not the prophet but the prophet's assistant. This looks like the ultimate insult. If a respected person travels a long distance and comes to your door to see you and you don't open it, that's disrespectful.

And not only did the servant go to the door, but he simply read the general instructions ordered by Elisha: "Go, wash yourself seven times in the Jordan, and your flesh will be restored and you will be cleansed" (verse 10).

At this, Naaman became furious and turned away in a rage. But he was being tested. He wanted healing on his own terms but would be met with the only path that God uses to make us whole: humility. And having humility means lowering our defenses. For Naaman, this meant a total rejection of the identity he had carefully built over the years. For us, it means the same.

The way of humility essentially says, *I don't take myself too seriously; I have no need to project myself as something I'm not; I don't need to be in control; I'm open to things that are beyond my experience or understanding.*

After much protesting, Naaman went back. He reluctantly agreed to the prophet's instructions to dip in the dirty Jordan River seven times. Seven. It's a number of wholeness.

He took off his armor. (Can you imagine the embarrassment of exposing his skin to the entourage?) He started to dip.

First dip—nothing.

Second dip—nothing.

Third dip—*nothing*.

Fourth dip—**nothing.**

Naaman was probably ready to give up. He thought it was a waste of his time.

But he dipped again.

Fifth dip—NOTHING!

Sixth dip—*NOTHING!!!!!!*

His servants were probably praying, "Oh, Lord, don't make us have to go home with this grumpy, unhealed man."

At the seventh dip, he came up out of the water, and his skin was soft like a baby's bottom.

On the surface, it looked as if nothing happened until the seventh time he dipped. But I believe that the seventh time was a manifestation of the healing and transformation that Naaman was already experiencing. His body was healed on the seventh dip, but his heart was being transformed on the first dip, when he set aside his entitled ways and humbly said yes to Elisha's instructions.

Naaman's transformation is a paradigmatic story for our own wholeness and the healing of the world. To be the kind of presence that makes acts like confession, forgiveness, and empathy possible, having humility is imperative. But how do we grow in this area?

HABITS OF HUMILITY

Like all the virtues, humility is not achieved by happenstance—it is cultivated. The humble person is one who repeatedly chooses the counter-instinctual way of vulnerability, honesty, and self-confrontation. The road to a life lived in this way requires a commitment to an ancient path. As we near the end of this chapter, I want to focus on two core habits of humility: praying the Jesus Prayer, and the habit of receiving correction.

Praying the Jesus Prayer

Humble people are aware of the ongoing need for mercy. They are conscious of their own weaknesses. They are mindful of their insidious personal contradictions. One of the ways this transformational awareness arrives is through the regular contemplative act of praying the Jesus Prayer.

The Jesus Prayer is an ancient prayer found in the Gospels that was most profoundly adapted by Christians in the Eastern Orthodox tradition. The prayer, very simply, is "Lord Jesus Christ, Son of God, have mercy on me, a sinner." These words (although shortened) are found in Luke's gospel in a parable of Jesus (see 18:9–14). The story went like this: One day, two men went up to pray in the temple. One was a reflection of self-righteousness; the other, of humility. This is important. Jesus reminds us that pride is most dangerous in religious contexts because it can look like godliness.

The self-righteous figure in this parable is a Pharisee. Whenever we hear about the Pharisees, it's usually in a negative context. In the church world, one of the worst comments you could make about someone is telling them they're acting like a Pharisee. That's a fight waiting to happen in the church lobby. But we can learn some things from the Pharisees.

The Pharisees were holy people who wanted every facet of their existence to point to their covenantal relationship with God. They were the moral, generous, upstanding members of the community. They shoveled the front of their neighbor's house when it snowed. They were on the community board. They were people of prayer.

In the Old Testament, the ceremonial washings were essentially required for only the priests. The Pharisees, however, took those rituals and applied them to their respective homes. They wanted their tables at home to be as holy as the table in the temple. They were religious overachievers, desperately trying to mark all common life as holy as the temple. The problem, however, was that in their zeal, they had a tendency of becoming self-righteous. In the telling of the parable, Jesus shows us the shadow side of their zeal.

The Pharisee came to worship and stood by himself and prayed. He stood by himself not because he was an introvert but because he was too good for everyone. The Pharisee then went into his prayer in verse 11: "God, I thank you" (so far, so good) "that I am not like other people" (*Oh, Lord*).

The Pharisee went on to make a list of all the people he's not like. He listed robbers, evildoers, adulterers, people who don't return the cart to the right spot at the supermarket parking lot (that might not be in the original text), and the tax collector praying near him in the temple. In fairness to the Pharisee, the people he listed were not allowed to handle the Torah. It came across as a curious prayer of gratitude by way of condescension. But Jesus highlighted this Pharisee because something was off in his heart. He came to church impressed with himself.

Jesus then introduced the tax collector. Tax collectors were despised for their complicity with the Roman government.

The tax collector, perhaps feeling great guilt due to his greed, had one simple prayer: "God, have mercy on me, a sinner" (verse 13). In that moment, Jesus said that the man who recognized his need for mercy went home in right relationship with God; the other didn't. In the recognition of his poverty—although he had plenty of material wealth—the tax collector was declared righteous by Jesus.

Christians throughout the ages have looked to this parable and used it as a framework for prayer and for loving well because this prayer is good for the soul. The prayer grounds us in our ongoing capacity to miss the mark. It calls us to receive Jesus's mercy desperately and joyfully.

In a blaming and scapegoating culture, the Jesus Prayer helps us confront our duplicitous ways.

In an attacking and shaming society, the Jesus Prayer grounds us in our own inconsistencies.

In a finger-pointing and judgmental world, the Jesus Prayer awakens us to the dark secrets we harbor within.

In so doing, the Jesus Prayer petitions the mercy of God, which is to lead us in petitioning mercy for others. After a while of praying, "Lord Jesus Christ, Son of God, have mercy on me, a sinner," we begin to pray, "Lord Jesus Christ, Son of God, have mercy *on him or her*, a sinner."

This doesn't mean that we can't name what's wrong in the world. The Jesus Prayer is not about establishing some false equivalencies. No, there are times when we must name the sins and confront people who have done wrong, but this prayer helps us do it with a different intent.

The practice of the Jesus Prayer is incredibly simple yet profoundly demanding. Here are a few ways I have tried to incorporate it into my life with God.

First, there are days when I sense the Spirit calling me to pray these words repeatedly throughout the day. I usually repeat the words "Lord Jesus Christ, Son of God, have mercy on me, a sinner" slowly and repetitively (not mindlessly) during set times of prayer. I often sit in a chair, close my eyes, and gently offer those words before God for five, ten, or fifteen minutes. I love this prayer because there is great power in the name of Jesus to heal and form our lives deeply in God. Additionally, this prayer positions me to name the ways I contribute to the fragmentation of the world. I need the mercy and grace of God just like everybody else.

Second, I often pray the Jesus Prayer before a difficult meeting. Throughout a given year, I find myself sitting across from someone over coffee or Zoom and having hard conversations. Oftentimes, the conversation is about something I said or did (or didn't say or do) that hurt someone. When I'm aware of the potential tensions that await me, I'll pray this for a few minutes. I do this because my default mode is to defend myself and shut someone else down with my words. But the Jesus Prayer roots me in the reality of my brokenness. This doesn't mean I don't offer my perspective on the matter, but by God's grace, my hope is to engage the person I'm sitting across from with a humble spirit, fully recognizing my own issues that need addressing.

Finally, from time to time, I take one or two of the words from the Jesus Prayer and soak in them. There are times when I get to *Jesus* and must stop at that name. The name reminds me that the God I'm in relationship with is one who is for me, not against me. Other times I focus on the words *on me*. Certainly, the world needs mercy, but lest I get caught up in my own righteousness, I'm stopped in my tracks. *Lord, have mercy—on me*. It's the very simplicity of this prayer that is its stumbling block. But God chooses the simple things of the world to confound the wise.

The Habit of Receiving Correction

I wish this weren't the case, but this is an ongoing necessary area of growth for me. The person being formed in humility is one who receives and even pursues correction. Why? Because the humble person recognizes the presence of blind spots.

Having humility enables us to live in freedom—the freedom from having to be perfect, knowing it all, and being it all. Humility requires us to admit that we don't see the full picture about ourselves, God, or the world.

The term *blind spot* is one that many of us are familiar with. When you drive, it is often the case that you can miss seeing a car that is next to you, as the side mirror doesn't pick it up. Many accidents have happened because of this. You couldn't see the whole picture. And this is cause not just for accidents on the road but for tragedies in our lives.

Relationships fail because of our blind spots. Misunderstandings occur because of our blind spots. Wars occur because of blind spots.

Humility says, *I know I have blind spots. Can you help me see?* Imagine for a moment if our relationships were characterized in this way?

Imagine if your boss came up to you and asked, "Can you help me be a better supervisor?"

Imagine if your mom or dad came up to you and said, "Help me be a better parent."

Imagine if your spouse approached you during dinner and asked, "How can I love you better?"

The world can be healed profoundly through these simple questions. Yet this attitude often goes missing from our lives because of how painful it is. But remember, the pain we feel usually stems from our false self still asserting control. God wants to heal us from this dominance, which is probably why Jesus spent much of his time healing the blind. Part of the reason for this is that the physical blindness many endured reflected the spiritual and cultural blindness of Jesus's day. Ironically, those who were able to truly see God at work (like Bartimaeus) were physically blind. In the Gospels, Jesus made it plain: "For judgment I have come into this world, so that the blind will see and those who see will become blind" (John 9:39). In other words, Jesus's ways reveal the ways God works: Those who can confess being blind are those who see; those who claim to see are truly the ones who are blind.

Practically speaking, the habit of receiving correction is a way of confessing the truth that we don't see everything about ourselves. On one level, we understand this. But on another, we don't. Humility says, *I need an outside perspective to help me see myself more accurately.*

And because the goal of a humble person is to be what God wants them to be, we must open ourselves up to another perspective and, from time to time, correction when needed.

But this is not easy.

Why do we have a hard time receiving correction? In a word, *shame.*

SHAME AND HUMILITY

Sometimes we don't like correction because, frankly, many people don't know how to give it. Beyond this, some of us grew up in an environment marked by perfectionism. And for others, we don't like correction because it painfully reminds us of our failures and shortcomings. When we are corrected, our insecurities often come to the surface. To be corrected exposes our gaps and reveals our weaknesses. Our fundamental identity is put into question. As a result, we resist correction. The resistance can be fueled by pride, for sure, but much more so by shame.

I remember preaching a message on shame a few years ago. When I stepped off the stage, one of our congregants, a native New Yorker, approached me and said, "You know, Pastor Rich, in the AA meetings I attend, shame is understood this way." And then he told me of the following acronym:

Should

Have

Already

Mastered

Everything

I had just preached the sermon, but in a New York second, God spoke right to me. How often have I carried self-condemnation for not mastering everything! This man's words pierced my heart and pushed me into the arms of Jesus and his gospel—the gospel that reminds us that we are not made whole by our mastery of everything; we are made whole in the love of God.

Without complicating this habit, there are a few questions we would do well to consider asking others, especially when disagreements, conflicts, and tensions surface. People growing in humility are open to other perspectives because they know that our vision is never perfect. Here are some questions to consider asking:

- How do you experience me?
- How might I have done that differently?
- Where do you see an area of growth for me?
- Where am I missing it?
- How can I love you better?

These questions arise out of vulnerability and usually require a person to feel safe in order for them to answer; but think for a moment how our lives would change if that became how we related to one another. Imagine our marriages, parent-child conversations, friendships, work relationships, and church communities permeated with this level of humble curiosity.

Humility, in the way of Jesus, truly can form love in us, make us whole, and, in God's power, begin to heal our suffering world.

CHAPTER 6

RESISTING REACTIVITY

Living as a Calm Presence in an Anxious Culture

In 2005, I sat next to my then fiancée, Rosie, with ten other couples who were preparing for marriage. I don't remember much from those series of premarital classes, but I've never forgotten one thing that was spoken with prophetic accuracy: At some point during the class, the instructor said, without a hint of humor, that it was going to take at least ten years to start learning how to be married. I thought, *How depressing*, and with playfulness—plus a bit of arrogance—I looked at Rosie and said, "Babe, it will take us two years max. Gimme a fist bump. Boom."

Well, the instructor was right. It has taken some years to learn how to be married. For us, *more* than ten years. I've come to understand why.

Much of the pain in our marriage has surfaced because it has taken me a long time to learn an important lesson: Rosie is not looking for someone to rescue her when she is in distress. I'm still learning that lesson, but I will say that I have made some good progress. In the first few years of our marriage, I had four modes of operation whenever Rosie was angry or sad. If I noticed her in a rough spot, I would try to make things better. My modes were questionable, however.

Mode one was to be a computer. After she voiced her anger or grief, I would immediately give her some calculated options. "Honey, you can [do this or that]. What do you think?" This was usually met with a stare.

Mode two was minimizing. "Babe, is it *that* bad? You sure you're not overreacting?" This was usually met with a more intense stare. (For those taking notes, this doesn't work.)

Mode three was to superimpose. "Darling, if that were me, this is how I would respond." Crickets.

Mode four was to get the heck out of there. Another terrible response. At this point, the fist bumps were nonexistent.

Well, in due time, I went to see a therapist to get help. I found myself personalizing her anger and grief. I thought it was my job to rescue her from difficult emotions and painful circumstances. This faulty thinking only made matters worse. I shared with my counselor how hard it was for me to help Rosie whenever she was angry or sad about something. What I would hear from him in response puzzled me.

"Rich, I want you to do something simple the next time Rosie is angry or sad." With an eager tone, I replied, "Name it, Doc."

"Whenever Rosie is sad or mad, I want you to be sad or mad with her." A bit puzzled, I pondered his words. I responded, "What else you got?" "That's it," he said. "Be sad with her. Be mad with her." I walked out of that session wondering if I could get a refund.

But he was right. What she needed—and I readily admit that I still struggle doing this well—was someone to be curious and compassionate with her—someone to join her without trying to save her. I went home, jotted down some notes in my journal, and waited for an opportunity to love her well in this way.

A few days later, I noticed Rosie was bothered by something. She was frustrated but not angry. But I thought, *This might be my moment—my moment to shine.* As she shared her frustration, the four modes were ready to be implemented, but I remembered what the counselor had said and how much I'd paid for that session. "Be mad with her. Be mad with her." I would say these words under my breath as she aired her grievances. When the moment was right, I interrupted her with disproportionate energy for the situation and shouted, "She said *what?*"

I would continue to show how angry I was until Rosie tried settling *me* down. I was ten seconds away from kicking furniture. I wasn't trying to put on a show, but I wanted to let her know that I was with her—albeit in way that didn't match the situation.

Even so, do you know what my wife felt at that moment? Loved.

CULTIVATING CALM PRESENCE

Granted, my example is not the best case study, but I learned something in the process. It's a lesson that has application across every relationship: Becoming someone who can remain present to oneself and to another, especially in times of disagreement or distress, is one of the most important things we can do to become whole.

Some have called this lesson self-differentiation. For our

purposes, let's call it calm presence. (From this point on, I'll be using the phrase *calm presence*. By it, I'm referring to self-differentiation.) It's to be the natural outflow of a life that is marked by humility and contemplative prayer. It's how love is formed in us.

I'm convinced that the most important skill needed in our world today is learning to cultivate calm presence. The cultivation of calm presence is the conscious and courageous decision to remain close and curious to ourselves and others in times of high anxiety. It's a concept birthed out of family systems theory.

In the 1950s, a psychiatrist named Murray Bowen sought to understand the ways our families of origin shape our lives and our connection—or lack thereof—to the world. One of the core tenets of family systems theory is the natural tendency people have to anxiously attach to someone on the one hand and anxiously detach on the other. The respective forces of togetherness and individuality foster certain personal and interpersonal dynamics that hurt relationships. Songs are written all the time about this.

For example, in 1997, I worked at Sony Theaters in Manhattan. To this day, I can proudly recognize dozens of songs that came out during that year, because they played nonstop throughout the theater. One of the songs that came out in 1997 was country artist LeAnn Rimes's song "How Do I Live." While romantic on one level, on another, it's a song for someone who is "fused" into someone else.

Two decades later, pop artist Selena Gomez came out with a song called "Cut You Off." There you have it. The two extremes of our society: *How do I live without you?* and *Cut you off.* These ideas capture the spectrum of attachment and detachment, togetherness and individuality, fusion and cutting off.

For some of us, we relate to others in such a way that we disappear into them, burying our ideas, opinions, and feelings for the sake of remaining close. For others, we assert our ideas, opinions, and feelings to such a degree that our individuality is prioritized over connection with others. Both approaches do not lead to the kind of wholeness we yearn for. What we need is the capacity to remain close—to ourselves and others.

Remaining Close to Ourselves

Calm presence requires emotional and spiritual closeness to ourselves. It's a way of life that takes seriously the feelings, dreams, preferences, and values that live within us. It's a way of life that listens to the prompts and stirrings of the Spirit within. This way of life can be very difficult to realize because for some of us, our feelings, dreams, preferences, and values were never taken seriously by others. Perhaps you came from a home that didn't see you as one worthy of thoughts or feelings. For far too many, children are to be seen but not heard within our homes. They are not given the dignity to name their frustration, articulate their preferences, and clarify—albeit in a limited way—their values. This lack of emotional freedom is often carried well into adulthood.

In our church, we teach various skills on emotional health. One of the skills is the practice of stating our preferences. It's remarkable how the words *I prefer* are not able to flow from the lips of so many people.

I remember meeting with a congregant named Evelyn who was having a hard time with her adult child who lived in the same house. She had much difficulty being clear about her values for a clean and tidy apartment. The problem was that her adult son didn't carry that value. When I heard Evelyn lament the situation, I gently asked, "Have you ever stated your preference and expectation for a clean and tidy house?"

She deflected, "Oh, he would never listen, Pastor Rich."

"Yes, but have you at least attempted?" I asked. Silence ensued.

She tearfully replied, "If I start speaking about preferences and expectations, I might offend him." I started to dig a bit deeper.

"Can you tell me about your childhood, Evelyn? Were you ever given space to share preferences without judgment?"

"No way," she replied. "Sharing preferences? My mother would never."

I replied with as much pastoral sensitivity as I could muster. "Yes, but you're no longer under your mom's roof. You have a voice. You have values. You have preferences. It's okay to share them." I prayed with her to have courage for a difficult but necessary conversation.

That day, she went home and very sheepishly stated her preference to her son in the clearest language she could muster. She was shocked to see how well he received it. For so many years, she had lived as if she didn't have the right to name her values. She carried the emotional system of her family of origin for decades. Maybe you've done the same. I know I have.

Ronald Richardson, an expert on family systems theory, noted something Murray Bowen had said: "Time and distance do not fool an emotional system."[1] Richardson then continued,

> We carry that emotional system with us as we move around the country. I have had a seventy-year-old counselee have the same reaction to his ninety-five-year-old mother that he had when he was a teen. Once these emotional patterns are established, we carry them with us wherever we go.[2]

Cultivating calm presence is about remaining close and present to ourselves. It's about slowing down to gain clarity on the things that matter within—but not *only* within.

It's here where many people get into trouble with this concept. In various trainings, I've highlighted the importance of naming one's values and stating preferences and such, and people hear this as license to blast someone with their newfound voice. The sudden empowerment people feel to "speak their truth" is done in ways that don't facilitate connection. Cultivating calm presence is about remaining close to not just ourselves but others as well (the second part of my working definition).

Remaining Close to Others

If remaining close to ourselves is difficult, remaining close to others can feel like an impossibility. The opposite of differentiation is reactivity, emotionality, and automatic functioning. These are the words that describe our world. We all have seen that the way of reactivity causes a severe lack of emotional connection. *Unfriending, blocking, muting,* and *canceling* are words that we are familiar with, yet the pace through which we carry out these acts is alarming. (Now, a word of wisdom. Remaining close to others who are hostile, abusive, manipulative, and so on is not what I'm suggesting. In those situations, we would do well to create wise and healthy boundaries to protect ourselves from that kind of treatment.)

Peter Steinke, a family systems theory expert, got to the core of remaining close to others. Among other indicators, he noted three signs of someone staying connected:

a. Maintaining a nonreactive presence with people who are reacting to you . . .

b. Resisting your own impulse to attack or cut off from those reacting to you, or to appease them to dispel their anger or frustration

c. Managing your own anxiety, not others' anxiety[3]

In other words, the person growing in cultivating presence is curious, courageous, and compassionate—three words that God wants to form in us for the healing of the world, and three words that are possible for those rooted in love. There's one situation that comes to mind that helped me see this up close.

CALM PRESENCE AMID POLITICAL DIVISION

On October 8, 2020, I made the mistake of opening an email late at night before going to bed. It was from one of our community-life pastors. She excitedly sent an email that filled me with anxiety:

Rich, I have an exciting update for the Faith &
Politics event we are planning on Zoom. Two of
our church elders will be in dialogue about why
they are voting differently! One is voting for
Trump, and the other for Biden. I'm so thrilled
they both agreed, and we are working with them
to prepare for the dialogue they will share at the
event in a couple of weeks.

With great, unshakable faith, I thought, *This is a terrible
idea! I know the election is less than a month away, but this is
not the time to have people in our church talk openly about why
they are voting in different ways.*

I was taken aback that these were the first words in my
head, but I kept on playing the scenario out. I thought of
everything that could go wrong: the awkward political talking points, the cleanup that would inevitably follow, the
angry emails from people who didn't like what was said at
the forum, and the many exasperating times we'd have to
say, "You're on mute."

Oh, me of little faith.

After reading that email, I had a hard time sleeping. Ultimately, we went on with the event. More than 150 people
from our congregation showed up on Zoom to participate.
I showed up, waiting a few minutes before I unmuted myself and showed my face on the screen. I still had reserva-
tions. After taking a deep breath, I unmuted myself and,
like a game-show host, brightly smiled and welcomed everyone to the event. I was anxious, but who could blame
me, right?

The year 2020 had already exposed cracks in our community. Through the painful convergence of crises—Covid-19,

political hostility, and racial injustice (fittingly, CPR for short)—I found myself regularly on edge. Many of the emails from congregants, especially the ones critiquing some of my sermons, felt like repeated judgment on my character. I would have "exit interviews," except I didn't know they were exit interviews at the time. People were leaving the church because of the intensity of the cultural moment. Staying connected was difficult. I'm sure you understand.

Polarization was surfacing in our church family in ways I hadn't seen before, leading me to wrestle with a set of questions: What does it mean to stay connected? How can we hold space with one another? How can we resist the emotional and relational cutoffs that seemingly mark the entire world? How can I move close to people who have very different visions of what human flourishing looks like? Do I have what it takes to listen deeply and offer an unanxious presence to those who don't see the world as I do?

These are the questions I reflected on almost daily, which led me to examine the gaps in my own life that contributed to the increasing divide in our world.

When the Faith & Politics event began, I welcomed everyone and gave a fifteen-minute talk on why spirituality and emotional health was so important in this arena. (It's often easier to teach it than live it.) After my talk, I handed the stage over to a young Black millennial congregant who would moderate the conversation between a Korean American man in his late forties and a Puerto Rican man in his midsixties. These men came from vastly different backgrounds, leading them to see the world in very different ways.

During the event, I found myself anxiously reading comments in the chat section from other congregants who disagreed with something one of the elders had said. I winced a couple of times when I heard an answer I didn't agree with. I realized my breathing was becoming constricted when a delicate topic was brought up. I noticed I didn't have many fingernails left to chew as the forum went on. But we did it. I saw three members of our community winsomely dialogue with each other. Did it solve all the tensions in our community? Of course not. But we caught a glimpse of what being rooted in love could look like.

IN TIMES OF HIGH ANXIETY

The third part of my working definition of self-differentiation has to do with anxiety. The language of anxiety is core to understanding calm presence. Anxiety is usually understood in terms of fear and timidity, but it is not so much about feeling afraid as it is an automatic way of functioning. Anxiety manifests in the instinctual response to an immanent or imagined threat. It's the opposite of careful, prudent, calm action and reaction. Anger, control, manipulation, avoidance, sarcasm, and distraction can all be expressions of anxiety. It flows through all of us, which is why paying attention to the anxious forces within and without us is critically important to developing calm presence.

It's relatively easy to remain close to myself and others in times of low anxiety. The true test comes when anxiety is high. The person growing in this area is constantly aware of the presence of anxiety, seeking to remain present for the sake of love.

To be this kind of person requires a level of individual and interpersonal curiosity, self-compassion, and the willingness to put boundaries on coerciveness. In other words, we venture to see ourselves and the other—whoever that other might be—as sacred beings deserving of care and respect. Yes, easier said than done.

The alternatives to calm presence are emotional fusion and emotional cutoffs, which dominate how we often relate to one another, whether we are discussing home finances, racism, or public-health crises. Emotional fusion is the subtle act of *disappearing into* another person. Our values, opinions, concerns, and fears are not given the kind of expression required for healthy engagement. It's a way of living that anxiously centers another's values, opinions, concerns, or fears without giving adequate attention to ourselves. Emotional cutoff is the polar opposite response, characterized by emotional distance, callousness, and a *disappearing from* another person. Whether we are disappearing into someone or away from someone, we have much work to do in developing calm presence instead. Thankfully, we can gain some help from Scripture.

CULTIVATING CALM PRESENCE: EXAMPLES FROM THE BIBLE

There's much we can learn from the Bible about cultivating calm presence. Although we won't find a chapter and verse in the Bible that speaks directly to the concept, there are a few instances that serve as helpful examples. Let me highlight three of them.

David and Saul

The interaction between David and King Saul in 1 Samuel 17 is a wonderful case study in calm presence. David demonstrated closeness to himself and closeness to Saul in a time of extreme anxiety.

In this story, the Israelites were once again in a battle with their noted rivals, the Philistines. The Philistines had the renowned giant warrior Goliath on their side. Goliath mocked the warriors of Israel, trying to lure them into a gladiatorial battle. But no one from Israel was saying yes to this invitation. (I wouldn't either.)

At this point, David, a young shepherd, came on the scene to deliver lunch to his brothers. As he distributed the cheese and bread, he overheard some of the soldiers of Israel. They reminded each other that whoever fought Goliath—and wins, of course—would receive great wealth, the king's daughter in marriage, and exemption from paying taxes. David's eyes grew large. He was willing to risk his life for this prize.

It's at this point we see an important moment of calm presence. King Saul heard of this courageous teenager and wanted to help him succeed. He gave his armor to David for him to put on before fighting. David did so but soon realized that it didn't fit. He prudently took it off and searched for stones to place in his slingshot. As everyone knows, he went on to defeat Goliath.

The armor-wearing moment is key for our purposes here. David didn't mindlessly go the route of distancing himself from Saul in the name of individuality. He was not callous toward Saul but tried on the armor. It was an act of openness, curiosity, and humility. David stayed in good connection with Saul. But if David went to battle in Saul's armor, he would have been slaughtered. So far, David had the "Remain close to others" part of calm presence down. But he also remained close to himself.

David had a history of fighting with his slingshot, so after trying on the armor, he realized that he stood a better chance if he fought the way in which he was accustomed. To remove Saul's armor in front of everyone was a courageous act that could potentially embarrass Saul since David was rejecting Saul's idea. But he was not controlled by the anxiety of the moment or by Saul's attempt to help. He was thoughtful and decisive.

The story ended well (for David and Israel), but things don't always look like this in the real world. Saul could have become defensive, angry, and embarrassed that David would take off his armor. Similarly, when we remain close to ourselves, in a principled, unanxious manner, the people around us might not respond well. But remember, calm presence is marked by low reactivity.

Aaron and Israel

In a less healthy example, Aaron, Moses's brother, demonstrated the lack of calm presence. God told Moses to go up the mountain to receive clear instructions as to how the people of God were to be formed (see Exodus 24:12). While up there, the Ten Commandments were given. Moses was away from the people for about forty days. During that time, they got very anxious. Perhaps they were thinking that Moses lost his way. Maybe his phone ran out of batteries or he slipped and fell. (He was more than eighty years old, after all.)

In their anxiety, they went to Aaron, looking for leadership. They demanded a god they could worship and put their trust in. Aaron said, "Okay." Just a few days prior, God had given them a command that said, "You shall not make any graven image; you shall not create an idol" (see 20:4). But anxiety will make you do some irrational things.

Aaron instructed the people to give to him their "gold earrings" (32:2). The gold rings were to be used for furnishing the Lord's tabernacle as a home to the Lord's presence with Israel. Instead, Aaron decided to bend to the people's demands and use the gold to make a statue of a golden calf for them to worship (see verse 4).

God heard about this and was furious.

Later on in the story, Moses approached his brother Aaron and said, "What did these people do to you, that you led them into such great sin?" (verse 21).

Aaron replied, in one of the more humorous responses in the Bible,

> You know how prone these people are to evil. They said to me, "Make us gods who will go before us. . . ." So I told them, "Whoever has any gold jewelry, take it off." Then they gave me the gold, and I threw it into the fire, and [*boom!*] out came this calf! (verses 22–24)

Aaron demonstrated anxious presence by his emotional fusion with the crowd. He was overtaken by their anxiety, leading to a serious lapse of judgment. He thoughtlessly acquiesced to their demands. Much of the conflict and lapses of judgment we experience are influenced by the anxiety of the system we are part of, whether it be a family, work, or church system. In the process, we don't live from a discerning, whole place.

Jesus and the Crowds

No one cultivated calm presence better than Jesus. He remained close to the Father, himself, and others in times of great anxiety. Although he consistently made decisions that puzzled people around him, he never asserted himself without also remaining close to others. He was clear about his call but compassionate with those who didn't understand, he was decisive in his decisions and forgiving toward those who couldn't stomach his ways, and he was resolute in his truth telling but opened his heart to all. Yes, it is true that Jesus reserved some of his harshest criticism for the religious establishment for the ways they disregarded the poor, but even in his words of rebuke, he wept over a city that had not discerned the presence of God among them. We need his example to navigate the most difficult, polarizing issues of our day.

CULTIVATING CALM PRESENCE
IN A REACTIVE WORLD

Whether we are discussing racism, politics, marital disagreements, or church conflicts, orienting ourselves to fostering calm presence contributes toward the wholeness we yearn to experience. But it takes work. For the rest of this chapter, I want to explore practices of calm presence. The practices I highlight will emerge out of one notable personal story at the height of tensions in early 2021.

The early months of 2021 felt like extended months from 2020. January became the thirteenth month of 2020. Just six days into 2021, we saw images in Washington,

D.C., we've never seen before. The Capitol was under siege. While many saw the insurrection as an act of courage and patriotic dissent, it was a watershed moment in the history of the United States.

I had a sermon already prepared for the upcoming Sunday, when I turned on the television to see images of people angrily storming the Capitol. As I watched, I sensed that I needed to write a new sermon. With just a few days of preparation, I wrote a sermon on our baptism and what our allegiance to Jesus meant in this moment. Like with most sermons of this nature, many people were heartened and relieved that I would name what I believed to be a significant danger to our witness to Christ. Others were infuriated that I would point a finger of blame and further divide our church through my sermon.

In the weeks that followed, I would learn of a few congregants leaving our church. A handful wanted to have Zoom conversations to share their frustration with my preaching. Anxiety was high for me. At one point, a significant leader in our church emailed me, asking for a two-hour meeting. Reading the email caused my heart to race, my thoughts to swirl, and my breathing to become constricted. But I set up the appointment.

Two hours before the meeting, I noticed I couldn't catch a satisfying breath. (This is one of the symptoms of anxiety I exhibit when under great stress.) Realizing that this was not the best way to enter the meeting, I went for a walk to try to gain some clarity. Why was I so affected by this upcoming meeting? What was happening beneath the surface? What perspective did I need in order to move beyond my emotional state?

While walking, I returned to a practice that has served me well in similar moments. I carefully named the deceptive messages that were hijacking my soul.

I stopped walking, sat on a bench on Queens Boulevard, and started to examine the messages. I explored the internal scripts lurking within. While on the bench, I compiled a list of stories I had been telling myself. Although I theologically and intellectually knew these stories were not true, until I was able to name them with specificity, they had me in their grip. I hurriedly entered the messages into my phone. The messages that came out were as follows:

1. When people disagree with me, it means I'm a bad leader.

2. If congregants and I are not on the same page, I'm doing something wrong as a leader.

3. I'm causing division by bringing up delicate issues.

4. Things will end in the worst way possible, and it will be my fault.

5. I need others to like me for me to be okay.

6. I need others to agree with me for me to be okay.

7. People who leave New Life expose my deficiencies in leadership.

When I looked carefully at these deceptive messages, I realized how dangerous they were. I also realized the degree to which I had been shaped by them in moments of conflict. I read them again, taking deep breaths and recognizing the falseness of each. Attempting to bring some level of objectivity to my brain, I wrote,

> Plenty of people disagreed with Jesus, and he was the best leader the world has ever seen. The New Testament documents plenty of examples of when the church wasn't on the same page. Why am I surprised when it happens to me? Jesus brought up delicate issues but could hardly be described as one who wanted to divide people. Many people will not like me or agree with me on much. That doesn't mean I need to obsessively center their perspectives.

I did all of this in an hour's time. I closed with five minutes of silent, contemplative prayer and walked back home to have the Zoom meeting. I was pleasantly surprised to see the presence I was able to carry into that meeting. I listened and spoke clearly about my theological values. The elusive satisfying breath didn't come during or after the meeting (although it returned a week later), but my soul was grounded in a different place. I've made plenty of mistakes when navigating conflict, but here, I was encouraged to see God at work in my life.

When I look back at this moment, I notice a few practices that helped me love well, especially someone who had a vastly different outlook on the world than I did. What I just shared in my story were the practices of emotional self-regulation, naming the messages, and speaking clearly.

PRACTICES FOR CULTIVATING CALM PRESENCE

Emotional Self-Regulation

Emotional self-regulation is the ability to collect ourselves in times of distress. When someone is not emotionally regulating, they function from a place of reactivity. The unregulated person is marked by bursts of anger, impulsive decisions, and obsessive rumination. In the story I just shared, I noticed my breathing becoming constricted. I needed an environment to help me get out of my head. Going for a walk and taking deep breaths enabled me to settle into my body. This is the core of self-regulation: paying attention to our bodies. Self-regulation is not suppression. It's not ignoring the very real emotional sensations coursing through our minds and bodies. It's not spiritualizing. It's the training of our minds and souls to resist the force of our impulses.

Some emotional-regulation practices include walking, concentrated breathing, writing, painting, meditating, and praying. Calm presence requires a centered person—not a robot, but someone who can emotionally adjust to the moment. In other words, this is not about getting people to change; it's about taking responsibility for our own functioning with another person. Listen, I can barely change myself! How in the world am I going to change someone else? But that's just it. I'm not called to change others; rather, I'm called to work to relate to them differently. Emotional self-regulation is about adjusting ourselves in such a way that keeps us present to ourselves, for the sake of presence with others.

The biggest challenge in our relationships is placing the

burden of change on someone else. It's infuriating and exhausting to live from this place. Self-differentiation is the commitment to paying attention to *our* actions, *our* reactions, *our* anxiety, *our* responsibility. Through self-regulation practices, we give our bodies and souls the care they need in order for us to relate to others from a unanxious place.

Naming the Messages

The second practice requires the careful exploration of deceptive messages. In the personal story I shared, after settling down, I was able to write a litany of statements that were not true. Once I was able to get more clarity about what was bothering me, I could look at the messages with some form of objectivity. We all carry deeply rooted messages in our souls, and unless we can excavate, behold, and then reject them, we will live controlled by lies.

The work of naming the messages can take a good deal of time but is critically needed for the sake of our wholeness and love. If you are having difficulty identifying what messages are trapped within you, that might mean you need planned reflection. The seven messages I listed while sitting on that bench didn't come out of nowhere. Because of my commitment to journaling, I had named a couple of them here and there. But in the intensity of the moment, I was able to synthesize them in a way that helped me see the lies I'd been believing.

The work of cultivating calm presence begins as we wrestle with our own faulty thinking before we come face-to-face with someone in conflict. As a matter of fact, our ability to name the messages that heap shame on us is what positions us to remain close to others.

Speaking Clearly

Calm presence is about learning how to speak. I'm not talking about syntax and proper conjunctions; I mean the kind of speech that promotes understanding, healing, grace, and connection. In Emotionally Healthy Discipleship (a ministry of New Life Fellowship), Pete Scazzero lists four qualities of healthy speaking (respectful, honest, clear, and timely). All of this creates the capacity not just to remain connected to others through compassionate listening but also to live and speak maturely.

To speak respectfully is to honor one another. It's to regard people as made in the image of God, deserving of non-condescending speech. Healthy speech is also honest. It's not marked by spin, exaggeration, or minimizing. It's truthful. It's also to be clear. Healthy speech calls for interior and exterior clarity. And finally, healthy speech is timely—that is, it makes adequate, appropriate room for meaningful engagement.

When I do this well, I am able to ground my perspective gently but firmly on values that are very important for me as a pastor. I am able to be clear about my position and can do so with a tone of respect and love. This doesn't mean we will all agree. Hardly. But it means that the way we disagree does not have to lead to divisiveness.

To be rooted in love is not to believe in a fantasy that we will agree on every matter, big or small. But it is to believe in the possibility that we can remain close to ourselves and each other in the most challenging of moments. The truth is, we will disagree; we will bump against each other; we will have conflicts.

But our conflicts need not uproot our love. In fact, those very conflicts can embody it.

PART THREE

EMBODYING WHOLENESS

CHAPTER 7

A BRIDGE, NOT A BARRIER

Healthy Conflict in Pursuit of Wholeness

Having a life marked by goodness, beauty, and kindness means we must face conflict and deal with it maturely. I wish there were another way, but unfortunately there is not. Every day, conflict awaits. Sometimes it begins with us. Sometimes it starts with someone else. Sometimes we avoid it. At other times, we attack our way through it. But conflict comes. Here are some examples:

- You're upset with your spouse, who constantly comes home late after work. But you say nothing. Why? Because you think you're being like Christ by not complaining. Instead, you are passive-aggressive and give your spouse the silent treatment.
- You think your boyfriend is careless with his words toward you. He can be quite critical, but you don't think he'd take it well if you brought it up. You rationalize, *He has lived through a lot. I don't want to add to his pain.* So you bite your tongue, holding tightly to the Bible verse "Love covers over a multitude of sins" (1 Peter 4:8).

- You read a post from a friend on Facebook that you think is insensitive. Because you feel called to speak truth, you send a sharp DM, calling her to repent. She unfriends you.

- A friend hasn't returned your phone call. You assume he doesn't care for you. Instead of approaching him, you reach out to another friend to complain. You arrive at all kinds of conclusions and refuse to pick up his call, just to make him feel what you felt. The relationship starts to deteriorate.

For some of us, we live our lives avoiding the *potential* of conflict due to debilitating fear. A person living this way often has a hard time finding their voice, refuses to disagree, or painfully becomes a chameleon to limit the possibility of conflict. For others, we avoid the *reality* of conflict. This person lies nonstop, refusing to acknowledge the elephant in the room. Still, for others, the only way to deal with conflict is to speak loudly and clearly until others change their ways. None of these approaches reflect the way of Jesus.

For me, working through conflict has been, and remains, a challenge. I know what it's like to lose sleep because of a difficult conversation that needs to be had. I know what it's like to carry anxiety because someone I love and care for sees an issue differently than I do. I know what it's like to get emails from people who are disappointed by something I said or didn't say. I know what's it's like to have to confront someone because of their bad judgment. I know what it's like to be confronted by someone because of *my* bad judgment. So let me tell it to you straight: There is no other way. Our bodies might be telling us to flee, but conflict can be a bridge to love. It need not be a barrier.

When engaging in conflict, I'm referring to a serious disagreement regarding a meaningful situation. To be clear, I'm not referencing abuse. I'm not advocating for you to remain in dehumanizing situations. I'm not encouraging perseverance in relationships marked by a clear violation of boundaries. I'm talking about the normal and often emotionally charged disagreements we have. And there are many, because to be human is to experience conflict. Let's normalize this. Conflict is not a sign of unhealth. It's unhealthy to *never* have conflict.

When couples come to me for premarital counseling, I usually ask them to tell me about their conflicts. From time to time, I hear, "We don't have any conflicts, Pastor. We just get along." I usually smile and start digging. My goal is not to create issues that are not there, but I need to help them look harder, as being in relationship is to open ourselves up to differences. This is true for everyone. Throughout our lives, we will face conflicts: conflicts at work and home, at church and in the neighborhood, with our roommates and with our children. The list goes on.

And don't forget that dealing with conflict is not a sign of immaturity; it's a reflection of the depth of our maturity in Christ. Most relationships don't last, because conflict, for many people, is a sign that something is wrong. What's wrong is expecting it to be otherwise.

We often project a romanticized vision onto relationships, which gets catastrophically torn to pieces when it's found to be wanting. A simple three-stage synopsis of relationships comes in handy here.

THE THREE STAGES OF RELATIONSHIPS

There are many ways to capture the three stages I outline here, but I have found the language of *heavenly, hellish,* and *holding the tensions* to be useful. Let's explore each of these briefly.

The Heavenly Stage

When relationships start or a new person joins a church community, it's often regarded as heavenly. In this pseudo and surface stage—which is necessary and unavoidable—everything is ideal. In dating relationships, especially early on, you see the best in each other. You just met him, but you love him. Do you know his last name? Nope. But you love him, nonetheless. Have you met her in person yet? Nope, just virtually, but you're sure you're going to marry her. In this heavenly stage, we are on our best behavior, and we see the good (or refuse to acknowledge the bad) of the other. I see this often in church settings as well.

I can usually tell who's new to our church community. They are the people who are usually euphoric about everything: the music, the people, the warmth, the values. They don't see anything wrong with our church. Part of me really likes this stage, but against my inclination to keep them in illusion, I often say, "Just stick around." Don't get me wrong—I absolutely love the congregation I pastor. The people are beautiful, warm, and welcoming. But like every church in the world, sooner or later there will be some conflict. The problem isn't the conflict; the problem is how the conflict is addressed. This is where things shift and we hit the second stage.

The Hellish Stage

This is a letdown period. You find out that the man you fell in love with doesn't know how to be emotionally present when you're in distress. You find out that the woman you're smitten by spends more time working than being with you. You discover that the people at the church have some views about life that rub you the wrong way. You find out that the pastor doesn't see everything the same way you do. I find out, as the pastor, that you don't see everything the same way I do. It's at this stage when people feel disheartened, disillusioned, and despairing. It's the stage when people break up, quit their job, or leave a church. It's the stage where we begin to see more flaws than beauty—a stage marked by greater impatience and frustration. It's the period when people decide to leave a relationship or community, abandoning relationship altogether, or go on to search for the elusive heavenly stage once again. The cycle, however, never ends, and we never grow, because we are after something that doesn't exist.

The renowned German theologian Dietrich Bonhoeffer captured it this way: "Those who love their dream of a Christian community more than they love the Christian community itself become destroyers of that Christian community even though their personal intentions may be ever so honest, earnest and sacrificial."[1]

The Holding-the-Tensions Stage

At this point, we recognize that the heavenly stage is delightful but not realistic. And we acknowledge that the hellish stage is very real but need not be resisted. In this third stage, we do the work of growing up. We consciously bury our illusions but retain open hearts. We don't impose an unrealistic standard on someone or the community but accept the mixture that is to be found within and between us. In this stage, we resist idealization and pursue intimacy—an intimacy formed by grace, love, and forgiveness. We begin to love as God loves us: without illusion. God sees us as we truly are and holds us close. In this stage, we attempt to do the same with others.

These stages of relationships are important to underscore because everyone experiences them to some degree. This is also true of the relationships we see in Scripture. The Bible is not a collection of stories of holy people who always love God and neighbor well; it's a collection of severely broken, sinful people poorly navigating through life and consistently encountering a gracious God. When seen in this light, the Bible is good news for all of us.

CONFLICT IN THE BIBLE

I absolutely love stories of conflict in the Bible. I read them with a smile on my face. I find consolation that the church has had drama from the very beginning. It's something I need to remind myself of regularly. You should too. There's one conflict that I want to highlight that's instructive for our own conflicts. It's found in Galatians 2:11–21. Paul, the author of the epistle to the church in Galatia, recalled an intense moment he had with the apostle Peter (also known as Cephas).

It's important to note that Peter and Paul are two of the

most known and revered disciples of Jesus. They are the pillars of the church in the New Testament. They were holy men of God. But holiness doesn't protect us from conflict. No matter how much we pray, read the Bible, fast, or give to the poor, we will not be insulated from conflict. I used to think that conflict was a sign of immaturity (sometimes it is), but most of the time it is a regular experience of humanity.

The story went like this. Paul approached Peter because he recognized a dangerous hypocrisy that endangered the powerful but fragile movement called the church. Paul wrote,

> When Cephas [Peter] came to Antioch, I opposed him to his face, because he stood condemned. For before certain men came from James, he used to eat with the Gentiles. But when they arrived, he began to draw back and separate himself from the Gentiles because he was afraid of those who belonged to the circumcision group. The other Jews joined him in his hypocrisy, so that by their hypocrisy even Barnabas was led astray. (verses 11–13)

The New Testament unveils lots of tensions between Jews and Gentiles—tensions of religious, cultural, and theological sorts. But remarkably, these differences were shown to be powerless before the Cross of Christ. In Jesus, a new way was established in relating to God and to one another. In Christ, the people of God were not in right relationship with him because of their cultural and religious observances but were made right through faith in Christ.

As beautiful as this good news was for those in the first century, it was particularly hard for many Jewish Christians because they maintained the belief that right relationship with God consisted of faith *and* maintaining Jewish religious practices. Some believed that faith in Jesus was necessary, but so was circumcision and a particular diet. Yes, put your trust in Jesus, but don't forget to observe all the holy days too. They felt that holding all this together is what made you right with God. As a result, salvation began to look like this:

Faith in Christ + Cultural and Religious Observance = Salvation

This salvation equation made it especially challenging for Jewish Christians to accept the eating habits of Gentile Christians. But look what happened.

One day, Peter was hanging around Gentile Christians. And don't you know it, but at Gentile Christian parties, you ate stuff you didn't eat at Jewish parties. On the menu at the Gentile parties were pork chops, ribs, Italian sausages, shrimp scampi, lobster, bacon, *pernil,* and all the rest.

Peter, knowing that no Jewish Christians were around, pulled up a chair and began to feast (see verses 12–13). He was having a great time, when some of the Jewish legalistic Christians (known as the Judaizers) showed up. They were particularly intent on maintaining the salvation equation I mentioned a moment ago.

When Peter saw them coming, he anxiously wiped the barbecue sauce off his chin, yanked the lobster bib off, and threw the food under the table, separating himself from the Gentiles. In this surprising gesture, he was letting the Gentiles know that they were not accepted by God because they ate those things. Ironically (and hypocritically), Peter made this judgment with greasy hands and food stuck between his teeth, but he judged them, nonetheless.

Paul heard of this hypocrisy and addressed Peter directly, opposing him "to his face" (verse 11). He rebuked his brother in Christ, showing him that by his actions at the table, Peter had been creating a dangerous hierarchy and rejecting the gospel truth that faith in Christ is sufficient for salvation. In short, Peter was leading people astray.

Paul went into what makes us right with God—and it didn't consist of what we eat but rather who we believe in. So, there you have it. Right before our eyes, we have an emotionally and theologically charged conflict in the church, and there's much we can learn from it, first being that healthy conflict requires confrontation.

HEALTHY CONFLICT REQUIRES CONFRONTATION

For some people, the word *confrontation* is scary. It's a word many of us want to avoid. It seems to communicate aggressiveness, anger, and troublemaking. But confrontation need not be a debilitating word. By confrontation, I simply mean that conflict requires face time. No, not the video feature on your phone (although it serves us well), but the mature act of addressing an issue with someone and resisting the temptation to spiritualize it away.

In the portion of Scripture I noted above, Paul wrote, "When Cephas came to Antioch, I opposed him *to his face,* because he stood condemned." Imagine for a moment if Paul, knowing how dangerous Peter's actions were for the life of the church, had ignored them altogether. We'd have a very different Christianity for generations to come. But Paul did the mature, loving thing: He confronted.

This simple act was quite revolutionary and countercultural. It's also becoming a lost art. In her book *Reclaiming Conversation*, MIT professor Sherry Turkle noted a troubling yet very common trend among families and conflict:

> I meet families who say they like to "talk problems out" by text or email or messaging rather than in person. Some refer to this practice as "fighting by text." They tell me that electronic talk "keeps the peace" because with this regime, there are no out-of-control confrontations. Tempers never flare. One mother argues that when family members don't fear outbursts, they are more likely to express their feelings.[2]

I clearly recognize the angst that many attempt to avoid through "electronic talk." The problem, however, is that an entire generation is being taught to move further away from each other in the name of peace. There's just too much of ourselves that goes missing through texting and emails. Turkle aptly noted,

> These days, the first generation of children that grew up with smartphones is about to or has recently graduated from college. Intelligent and creative, they are at the beginning of their careers, but employers report that they come to work with unexpected phobias and anxieties. They don't know how to begin and end conver-

sations. They have a hard time with eye contact. They say that talking on the telephone makes them anxious. It is worth asking a hard question: Are we unintentionally depriving our children of tools they need at the very moment they need them?[3]

The act of confrontation is excruciating for several reasons:

- Many of us come from families that never learned how to navigate conflict. In some homes, it was addressed by ignoring, by running out of the house, or through violence.
- Some of us come from cultures and ethnic groups that frown upon directness. As a pastor of a church with roughly 30 percent of people from all parts of Asia, I've repeatedly heard how especially difficult this work of confronting can be in other parts of the world.
- Some of us have personalities that are particularly wired against confrontation.
- Many have been taught—explicitly and implicitly—that the Bible is more about forgiving than confronting.
- It is unnerving to sit before another person and communicate hurt, misunderstandings, and requests for change.

All these things are true. But in my pastoral experience, I'm keenly aware that confrontation is not a challenge for some of us but for most, if not all, of us. I've seen it happen with baby boomers and millennials, with well-educated and barely educated people, with Whites, Latinos, and African

Americans. I've experienced it repeatedly in my own life too. But you can do it. You can have these difficult conversations.

There's a liberating sentence I've come across that has helped me do the work of confrontation. The original context of the statement was not about confrontation but rather the felt sense of shame. It seems to me that there's lots of overlap here. In his book *The Soul of Shame*, Curt Thompson named the felt sense of shame and a corresponding internal message. Why does shame imprison us? Thompson noted that one reason is we internalize this script: "I do not have what it takes to tolerate this moment."[4]

That one line has helped me a good deal. Similarly, the message in our brains when confrontation becomes necessary is often "I do not have what it takes to tolerate this moment." But that is a lie. Are these moments difficult? Without question. Can we get through it? Absolutely. I've had to repeat the opposite of this quote from time to time when entering a conversation in which I needed to address conflict: "I *do* have what it takes to tolerate this moment."

Another key thing I've learned over the years is the importance of understanding triangulation and the harmful effects it has on our lives and relationships. Having face time is important, but the temptation to triangulate is ever-present.

Triangulation

Family systems expert Edwin Friedman wrote,

> The basic law of emotional triangles is that when any two parts of a system become uncomfortable with one another, they will "triangle in" or focus

upon a third person, or issue, as a way of stabiliz-
ing their own relationship with one another.[5]

The forming of triangles is a natural and potentially
healthy act. Insofar that the third person "brought in" fos-
ters mature processing and (when appropriate) encourages
the direct addressing of the issue, the forming of this trian-
gle can be a great gift. The problem is that often triangles
work against healthy confrontation. They become ways to
pour out anxiety on someone other than the source.

As a pastor, I'm often brought into conflicts. Sometimes
someone meets with me and because they met with me,
they don't think they have to confront the person they have
the issue with. At some point in the pastoral counseling session, I ask, "So, when are you having that conversation?"
The response is usually a blank stare. The person thinks the
issue is resolved because they got it off their chest. But
there's a difference between diffusing anxiety and living
maturely.

Triangulation, in many instances, is talking to everyone
about the problem except the person we need to speak to.
We see this in the famous Mary-and-Martha story.

In Luke 10:38–42, Jesus and his disciples paid a visit to
Mary and Martha. The two sisters couldn't have been more
different. Mary had a contemplative bent to her life, while
Martha was the activist. Martha probably saw Mary as an
under-functioner. Mary probably saw Martha as a worka-
holic. Jesus got to their home and Mary ran to sit at his feet,
taking on the position of a disciple. But there was much
work to do to feed Jesus and his friends. Martha was brew-
ing the coffee, setting the table, and keeping an eye on the
pot roast. Then she peeked over and saw her sister enrap-

tured by Jesus's words, and she lost it. There's where the triangulation surfaced.

In her exasperation, Martha came to him and asked, "Lord, don't you care that my sister has left me to do the work by myself? Tell her to help me!" (verse 40). (Side note: When you start bossing Jesus around, you're not in a good emotional space.) Martha went directly to Jesus, asking him to step in and resolve the anger and frustration she felt against her sister. Jesus didn't take the bait. Instead, he identified the anxiety and anger she carried.

What Martha needed then was the emotional where-withal to address her sister calmly but directly. Would things have changed? I don't know. But that approach would have been a better option than trying to get Jesus to do her dirty work.

Similarly, you might have come from a family in which parents—in the same home—would say, "Go tell your father . . ." or "Go tell your mother . . ." To be triangled into that kind of space is emotionally unfair. The work of addressing conflict and negotiating our differences requires us to grow in maturity—to do the hard but necessary work of "face-timing."

But face time alone will not solve our problems. It's common, especially for Christians, to hear Matthew 18:15–16 quoted when there's conflict within a community. In this passage, Jesus says,

> If your brother or sister sins, go and point out their fault, *just between the two of you*. If they listen to you, you have won them over. But if they will not listen, take one or two others along, so

that "every matter may be established by the testimony of two or three witnesses."

Jesus teaches face-timing as well, but what goes missing from our lives is how to be in that space when we get there. I've heard plenty of stories where somebody went to their brother or sister alone and when they got there, it all went downhill. So, let's nuance this a bit. Yes, we are to go directly to the person with whom there is conflict, but what do we do when we get there? The answer is rather simple but requires much of us.

HEALTHY CONFLICT REQUIRES
HEALTHY SPEAKING

I mentioned in the previous chapter how important healthy speaking is. I want to say a few more words to capture more nuances. It's remarkable that within the first few years of our lives, we can string together words, eventually forming coherent thoughts. As we continue to age, the words we weave demonstrate poignancy and astuteness. Yet for all the words we learn and sentences we expertly knit, there's still an aspect of speaking that goes deeper than conjugation and fine articulation. I'm talking about soul-speech.

I've met highly educated and accomplished people who communicated for a living before large crowds but were rendered mute when it came to speaking with a simplicity of soul. I can identify. When we are attempting to explore hurt, disappointment, or frustration, we don't need an expansive trove of multisyllabic words; we need plainness of

heart and clarity of speech. Over the years at New Life Fellowship, we have worked hard to nurture a culture of
healthy speaking. There are a couple of especially important
skills that have emerged from the Emotionally Healthy Relationships course we offer, but I will focus on the critical
one of clean fighting.

Clean Fighting

Before we talk about clean fighting, let's discuss its opposite.
Dirty fighting is the default for most of our families and,
consequently, our lives. By dirty fighting, I'm not referring
to slinging food at each other in the heat of battle (though,
certainly, this would indeed be dirty); I'm referring to the
ways we engage with each other that disregard our own
experiences or diminish others through our speaking.

Here are a few examples of dirty fighting tactics:

- the silent treatment
- lecturing
- condescension
- name-calling
- sarcasm
- avoiding
- hitting
- passive-aggressive behavior

The list goes on.

In place of this very normal but harmful way of interpersonal engagement, the way of clean fighting offers the possibility for honesty, integrity, respect, attunement, and
healing. Addressing conflict cleanly might feel like a new
language is being learned. In truth, you are learning some-

thing new. You are being invited to speak from your soul—the vulnerable, tender, animating part of yourself that tends to be hidden under the hard exterior of anger. What I will highlight here offers helpful language to begin the journey of clean fighting and soul-speech. As you practice it with intentionality, you'll find yourself growing in interior freedom and opening the possibility for greater relational health.

Pete and Geri Scazzero list a series of sentence stems to help prompt wise and honest speaking. If you're experiencing conflict, hurt, or a misunderstanding, take some time to slowly give expression to what's in your heart.

Steps to a Clean Fight

1. Ask for permission. State the problem.
   "I notice . . ."

2. State why it is important to you. "I value . . ."

3. Fill in the following sentence: "When you . . .
   I feel . . ."

4. State your request clearly, respectfully, and specifically.[6]

At this point in the skill, the listener would be invited to respond. (I will address the importance of listening in the next section.) The listener states how much of the request he is willing to do. The speaker then agrees with the listener or offers an alternative. In some cases, it is helpful to write down what has been negotiated and review it in a couple of weeks.

All this can sound wooden and unrealistic. Conversations are not as tidy as this skill can seemingly communicate. But the goal of learning the skill is to familiarize yourself with particular words to make your speech reflect internal clarity. Phrases like *I notice, I value,* and *I feel* go a long way in connecting with others. To state a request with clarity and respect is also an affirmation of your dignity and an act of love.

HEALTHY CONFLICT REQUIRES CAREFUL LISTENING

One of the questions I frequently hear is *What happens when my speech is healthy but the person listening is not?* It's an important question. My goal is not to paint a romanticized image of relationships. It is indeed very common, and quite frustrating, when there is this kind of relational imbalance. However, let me offer a few words to those who have a hard time truly listening, followed by a word to those in relationship with someone who doesn't listen well.

To those who have a hard time listening, I count myself among you. As I noted in my chapter on humility that we can be so bent on protecting an idealized image of ourselves that we refuse to step into the world of another person.

I remember the first time Rosie and I tried this clean-fighting skill. We were in our late twenties. The issue was one I imagine occurs in many homes. Rosie was frustrated by my lack of cleanliness after shaving. She worked the skill to perfection:

> **Rosie:** Honey, can we have a conversation about something that's bothering me?

Rich: [thinking to myself] *Oh dear Lord, what is this going to be about?*

Rosie: I notice that after shaving, you tend to leave a mess on the sink.

Rich: [deep sigh and long eye roll]

Rosie: I really value a clean bathroom, and it means a lot that we are on the same page with this.

Rich: Yep.

Rosie: When you continue to ignore my requests for a clean sink, I feel hurt and ignored.

Rich: [staring at the floor]

Rosie: My request is that you would fully clean the sink with the wipes we have after each shave.

The first time we practiced this skill (we had a coach to help us), I was so offended. I began to defend myself, highlighting all the other things I do in the house: washing the dishes, sweeping the floor, and throwing the trash out. I was not present with her. It took a good amount of reframing from our coach to help me step out of myself and into Rosie's world. I learned very quickly how enslaved I was to protecting my ego.

If you have a hard time being one who listens with an open heart, the best thing you can do to overcome this is internalize the love of God. We are all prone to make mistakes. But the hallmark of someone who is growing in love is one who can listen non-defensively.

That night we made some progress, but Rosie would

need to repeat her request again. When her request came forward without blaming but with a rearticulating of her value, I began to pay closer attention to the bathroom sink. It didn't happen overnight, but progressively I started to pay more and more attention to my ways. For several years now, after shaving, I'm leaving the sink cleaner than how I found it.

Listening well is a refusal to allow self-righteousness to distort our interactions. It's a willingness to open ourselves up to blind spots, knowing that we stand in need of grace every single day. Defensiveness is often a subtle but blatant rejection of our humanity and, consequently, a rejection of God's grace. Experiencing grace requires our walls to come down.

To those who are in the difficult situation of relating to someone who doesn't listen well, let me offer some ideas. First, recognize that their refusal to listen is a sign of a deeper issue. People in our lives don't normally resist listening because they enjoy being combative. In many cases, they just haven't been able to live from a deeper center of loving union with God. When I meet people who demonstrate difficulty in this area, I try to remind them of their belovedness. Knowing ahead of time that someone's lack of listening likely stems from something deeper might help you relate to them with more compassion.

But again, I'm not here to romanticize these things. In some cases, the best course of action is to invite a third party in to bring greater objectivity. Consistent refusal to listen might also require a boundary to be set or for a total rethinking of the relationship. These are painful realities, but by God's grace, we can all grow in speaking and listening with greater love and maturity.

HEALTHY CONFLICT REQUIRES THE TABLE

These new skills and practices are essential, but they will fail us if we are not immersed in the life of God. Love is something God forms in us as we open ourselves to the bottomless reservoir of grace. For the Christian, this reservoir is prominently available in the bread and the cup.

Holy communion is one of the great reenactments and catalysts for reconciliation. At the table, we are once again invited to live in the center of God's ever-expansive love. The table is not a reward for good behavior but a gift for the broken. In receiving the bread, we hear Jesus saying, *This is my body, broken for you.* In receiving the cup, the Lord says, *This is my blood, poured out for you.* At the table, we are tangibly granted the reassurance that God's love comes to us. But this is not all that is taking place. The table calls us to horizontally reenact this good news. As Jesus says, freely we have received; freely we give (see Matthew 10:8).

For the Christian, one of the reasons receiving the elements of the bread and cup is foundational for our lives is our fractures. Yet, paradoxically, the broken, fractured body of Jesus is the ground of all wholeness.

At New Life, we celebrate at the Lord's table the first Sunday of each month. There are months when I offer the bread and cup to the congregation, and other months when fellow pastors and elders share in this task. But I'll never forget one Sunday in particular.

I preached a sermon, led our church in a prayer of confession, and stepped down to hold the elements before my brothers and sisters. Our church is somewhat large, so various pastors are assigned sections in the sanctuary to distribute the bread and cup. As I stood offering the elements, I recognized a congregant standing in line at my section. I had experienced some conflicts and disagreements with this person. My first thought when I saw him was, *Of course you would do this to me, Lord.* Little by little, the man moved toward me. I could very easily go through the motions, offering him the elements with a cold heart. But the Holy Spirit began to soften my heart in the forty seconds it took for the congregant to get to me.

When he stood in front of me, I spoke his name, followed with, "The body of Christ, broken for you. The blood of Christ, poured out for you." He offered a sincere word of thanks and smiled as if he was in on what was happening within me. Later that day, I reflected on that moment. Did our conflicts magically disappear? No. Did we see everything the same because I offered him the body and blood of Christ? Nope. But something shifted in my soul.

And this is the point: Our conflicts are normal. Our disagreements are real. But so is the grace of God.

I wish I could tell you that all our conflicts will come to a peaceful end. But you and I both know that's not true. We wound others and are wounded by others. These wounds have a way of tearing us apart, from the levels of our families to the rifts that grow between nations.

But are we doomed to merely suffer the fallout and agony of this conflict? Praise God, no. Christ has led us to a better way.

CHAPTER 8

THE GIFT OF FORGIVENESS

Honestly Breaking the Cycle of Offense

There are few guarantees in life, but one thing is inevitable. At some point, someone will hurt you. You will be insulted. Someone might leave you when you need them most. You will be disappointed. You might even be betrayed. Perhaps, God forbid, you or I will suffer violence or another unthinkable violation of our personhood. When this experience comes our way, there are two agonizing options before us: to forgive or not to forgive. Whatever you choose to do, this will most likely be a painful undertaking.

This issue of forgiveness affects all of humanity, no matter our age. It surfaces in playgrounds all over the world after school. It shows up in boardrooms in major corporations. It confronts us in our homes every day. And, of course, we must wrestle with it in our churches. How we deal with forgiveness is important. I'm reminded of times of prayer I had some years ago with my daughter, Karis, who was four at the time.

Each night, Karis and I would spend time talking about our day. Afterward, we would recite the Lord's Prayer together. It took many weeks for her to memorize the words, but in the process, unbeknownst to her, her version was a hilarious prayer that reflected most of our lives:

> Our Father in heaven, Halloween be your name.
> My kingdom, I will be done.
> Give us today our daily trespasses.
> And forgive us our trespasses, as *we forget* those who
>   trespass against us.

Her prayer cracked me up every night.

Most of us have prayed this prayer in some way before. If we're honest with ourselves, we'll admit that we might have said the right words but our hearts were praying something altogether different. And understandably so, because forgiveness is a crucifixion. It often feels like a human impossibility, particularly in a world that uproots love.

TO FORGIVE OR NOT TO FORGIVE

Few things are more controversial, scandalous, and beautiful than an act of forgiving love, especially one of a public nature. Consider such an act in a courtroom in 2018 in Dallas. Earlier that year, an off-duty police officer—a thirty-year-old White woman named Amber Guyger—entered the apartment of a twenty-six-year-old Black man named Botham Jean and fatally shot him. She stated that she had entered his apartment accidentally, thinking it was her own.

When she saw the man in *his* apartment, she opened fire, believing he was a burglar. Amber would be convicted and sentenced to ten years in prison.[1]

At the close of the trial, there was a surprising moment of mercy extended to Amber from Botham Jean's eighteen-year-old brother, Brandt. After the jury sentenced Amber, Brandt asked the judge if he could give a hug to the woman who killed his brother.

He would go on to explain,

> I don't want to say twice or for the hundredth time what you've or how much you've taken from us. I think you know that. . . . If you truly are sorry—I know I can speak for myself—I forgive you, and I know if you go to God and ask Him, He will forgive you.[2]

When Brandt hugged Amber, the world responded with a myriad of reactions. Some were outraged that this gesture of forgiveness and warmth was extended, citing that had the tables been turned, hugs, forgiveness, and comfort would not be acts seen in a court of law. Others praised the act of forgiveness, seeing it as a powerful demonstration of the very essence of Christianity. In the process of this visceral public debate, much was lost. The act of forgiveness was once again seen through dualistic, either-or eyes. The options were simple: wholehearted, immediate forgiveness on the one hand, or principled unforgiveness on the other.

As I contemplated the hug seen around the world and engaged in conversation on social media with others, I began to wonder if a third way could be imagined for this situation and for our time. A way not characterized by sappy moderate sensibilities or by cheap reconciliation but rather marked by lament, anger, grace, *and* forgiveness.

To begin to make sense of the polarizing nature of this consoling hug and word of forgiveness, it was important to name the racial dynamics that create legitimate dissonance among Black men and women. Why is it hard for many to see a Black man comfort and extend grace to a White woman convicted of murdering his brother? Why couldn't some just see this as an extension of the gospel of grace? Why did this act expose fractures in our society? In a very real way, this is the fruit of racial oppression throughout the centuries in the United States.

Black men and women have been consciously and subconsciously taught to quell their anger, grief, and outrage in place of forgiveness. Scripture historically has repeatedly been used as a tranquilizing agent, creating cultures of obligatory obeisance, quieting any legitimate expressions of anger and disorientation. It becomes permissible and even expected in this context to gnosticize forgiveness, splitting the spiritual act of it without concurrently holding on to the bodily feelings of rage and grief. But who said forgiveness can't hold all these realities together?

In the book of Psalms, we consistently see the wide range of emotional processing on display as psalmists name their fear, anger, and puzzlement while offering petitions for God's grace and forgiveness. The question is not whether forgiveness is the right thing to do. The question is, In a racialized, politicized, and polarized society, can we hold together all the layers of pain while pronouncing grace over another?

WHAT ARE WE DOING WHEN WE FORGIVE?

Exploring forgiveness is a massive undertaking, but at the core of it, there are interpersonal and interior elements that must be held together. Interpersonally, forgiveness is a gift. It is bestowing to an underserving person an act of grace. The forgiving person possesses a generosity that confounds the world. As Croatian theologian Miroslav Volf has noted, our society is one marked by selling and buying, not giving and receiving.[3] Forgiveness is scandalous in our culture because we are overtly and covertly shaped by violence, retribution, and exclusionism. Instead of marking us by this way of being, forgiveness extends the gift of unmerited grace.

Volf also noted the essence of the interpersonal nature of forgiveness. He wrote, "By forgiveness, we release [the offender] from the burden of their wrongdoing."[4] To forgive is to cancel the debt owed, to forego retribution, to say no to revenge. It's the clear recognition of wrongdoing but the refusal to continue the cycle of offense. In the act of forgiveness, we imagine God in glorious ways, for he is one who delights in forgiveness.

The act of forgiveness is primarily interpersonal, but it also has a profound interior component as well. Forgiveness is inner freedom from allowing the wound inflicted from another to be the primary and permanent point of reference from which we relate to the world. In practicing forgiveness, we are granted a new lens to encounter others. Unforgiveness doesn't merely inform the way we relate to the person responsible for the offense; it metastasizes to the point where other relationships are filtered through previous experiences.

Forgiveness is a miracle of God's grace that reflects his

character in profound ways. It's the call of every Christian to move toward forgiveness, releasing our debtors and entrusting them to God's love and justice. This is often a lifetime of work—work we must give ourselves to if we and the world are to be rooted in love. Work worth our time and energy.

Consider a world where people are routinely requesting and offering forgiveness. Think about the joy in our homes that would uproot resentment. Try to visualize relationships not marked by defensiveness and contempt. Ponder the amount of stress you wouldn't have to carry, because the weight of bitterness and self-protection would not be necessary. It's a beautiful vision of the good life, yet it's not easy to get there.

Consider Jesus's first disciples.

FORGIVEN BUT STILL IN PRISON

In Matthew 18, we come across one of those gospel stories where Peter is trying to show off to Jesus (see verses 21–35). It's a recurring theme. Peter was the classic over-achiever and often sought to demonstrate to Jesus how spiritually impressive he was.

In this story, Peter approached Jesus and asked, "Lord, how many times shall I forgive my brother or sister who sins against me? Up to seven times?" (verse 21). Some biblical scholars say that it was common teaching in Israel that forgiveness could be limited to three times a day.[5] Peter, perhaps understanding this idea and being very generous, doubled it and added one more time for good measure. I imagine Peter smugly taking a sip of coffee and winking at his fellow disciples: "Up to seven times, Jesus?"

Instead of giving him a fist bump and some praise, Jesus replied, "I tell you, not seven times, but seventy-seven times" (verse 22).

Peter must have spit the coffee right out of his mouth.

Jesus then began to tell a parable to make his point (see verses 23–35, NKJV). The parable was about a man who owed his boss—the king—ten thousand talents. In those days, the talent was the largest unit of currency. Think of it as the hundred-dollar bill.

A talent was roughly worth twenty years of services, so this servant owed the king two hundred thousand years of labor. The people listening in on Jesus's story would understand that he was being humorous but also serious. It's like he was saying that this man owed one gazillion dollars.

The theological message is important. The debt that the man owed his boss is like the debt that we owe God. Our efforts to be in good standing with him are never adequate. We don't have the money in the bank to make it happen. The man in our story felt that way. When he saw his boss, "the servant fell on his knees before him. 'Be patient with me,' he begged, 'and I will pay back everything'" (verse 26). Everyone listening to Jesus knew that it was impossible for the servant to pay back everything. That's the point here.

Jesus went on to say that the servant's master took pity on the man, canceled the debt, and let him go. You would expect that at that very moment, after that encounter with his generous and forgiving boss, the man would have gone running in the street. I imagine the guy hugging strangers ·

in the neighborhood and jumping and kicking his heels. What a gift he'd received.

This is a story of unbelievable forgiveness, magnanimous mercy, and scandalous generosity. What a beautiful ending. But read on. There's a shocking twist.

The forgiven man walked out of the boss's office and suddenly spotted a co-worker who owed him money. The co-worker approached him with open arms to greet him, but the forgiven man remembered something. Six months ago, they had been at Starbucks together standing in line. The co-worker left his wallet at home and needed seven dollars for a grande caramel macchiato. The forgiven man generously paid for him. But now he remembered that his co-worker owed him seven dollars.

The forgiven man proceeded to grab his co-worker by the collar, choked him, and said, "Where's that seven dollars you owe me, you rat? You owe me!" (see verse 28).

The co-worker repeated the same line this forgiven man had *just* said to his boss: "Be patient with me, please." But the forgiven man refused. As he was choking his co-worker, a nearby stranger took out his phone and began to document it all on social media. (Stick with me here.) The video went viral, and the boss who forgave gazillions saw it. He immediately threw the once forgiven man in prison.

One of the lessons we learn from this parable is that you can be forgiven but still be in prison. Notice in this parable that true freedom is not just in receiving forgiveness but in allowing that grace to flow through us to others. The man in the story refused to allow his forgiveness to overflow to others, and as a result, he remained in bondage. This is what unforgiveness does to us. It puts us in a prison of our own making. But God wants to set us free.

Before arriving at this place of freedom, however, there are few things to say to nuance forgiveness.

WHAT FORGIVENESS *DOESN'T* MEAN

Forgiveness must be treated with care because it can be a tool of manipulation ("You better forgive me or else") or lead us to deny parts of our humanity in a rush to forgive. This is a short-circuiting of the process and not what forgiveness is about at all. There are at least four aspects of forgiveness that are important for us to wrestle with as we walk the journey toward forgiveness.

Forgiveness Doesn't Mean Forgetting

Many people look to a passage in Isaiah where God "forgets" the sins of his people: "I, *even* I, *am* he who blots out your transgressions, for my own sake, and remembers your sins no more" (Isaiah 43:25).

The argument often goes like this: God forgets my sin; to be like God is to forget other people's sins too. Now, a couple of things. First, to say that God forgets our sins is metaphorical language to help us understand that God doesn't hold our sins against us. But make no mistake: God, the all-knowing One, remembers our sins. This is what makes forgiveness so powerful. In the act of forgiveness, God's memory is not wiped clean like a laptop we want to refurbish, nor should we be expected to live with a sudden case of amnesia. God still has memory of our sins and, in mercy, doesn't hold them against us.

Second, remembering another's sins is helpful, especially when the possibility of hurt and abuse is real. By remembering, you create necessary boundaries to avoid repeat offenses. But by forgiving, you extricate yourself from the cycle of revenge.

Forgiveness Doesn't Mean There Are No Consequences

When God forgives us, the consequences of our sins are not necessarily sidestepped. Our choices have very real consequences, and an act of divine forgiveness doesn't necessarily remove the impact of our misguided ways. Similarly, forgiveness doesn't mean that justice is rendered obsolete. Forgiveness and justice are not mutually exclusive.

Forgiveness Doesn't Mean You No Longer Feel the Pain of Grieving

As a pastor, I'm often asked by a troubled congregant why they still feel the pain of grief even after forgiving someone who inflicted harm. The answer is simple: We are human beings who feel deeply. Forgiveness is not medicine that heals past pain and inoculates us from feeling new waves of it. Forgiveness and grief are often held together. If you're feeling the pain of what someone has done, that doesn't mean you haven't forgiven that person; it means that wound was deep.

Forgiveness Doesn't Always Mean Reconciliation with Another Person

The glorious forgiveness handed to us through Christ results in our reconciliation with God. This is not necessarily how it always works in human relationships, however. There are times when another person doesn't have the ability to be in healthy relationship. And, frankly, there are times

when the wound is so deep that full restoration of relationship is not possible. That is when we must grieve the losses
that come our way.

FORGIVENESS IS A JOURNEY

When I think about the journey of forgiveness, I think
about the literal journey my father took in Puerto Rico. In
2006, after nearly fifteen years of not seeing his father, my
dad wanted to confront some of the areas of his own life,
find his father, and choose the way of forgiveness.

My paternal grandfather was a great athlete but a man
with significant parenting gaps. He was a womanizer, abuser
of alcohol, and absentee father. For more than three decades, my father would live with deep resentment and unforgiveness toward my grandfather. It would eat him up in
many ways. But one day he decided to take a trip to Puerto
Rico to see his father and pronounce forgiveness over him.
My dad told this story on Facebook in 2006 on the day my
grandfather died in 2016:

> I spoke with my wife and told her I needed to
> find my father. I needed closure and desired to
> forgive him personally. After much thought, I de-
> cided to go on a journey to Salinas, Puerto Rico.
> I went there blind, not knowing exactly where he
> lived. The last time I had seen him was fifteen
> years ago. It took me almost a full day to find
> him. I had to ask many people, including the po-
> lice department, for direction.
>
> After a long journey, I finally reached his

home, and he arrived soon after I did. When he saw me, he was in shock. He said, "Ricky? Is that my Ricky?" I said, "Yes, Father," and he started crying uncontrollably like a baby.

He invited me in, and we talked well into the next morning. I was a man on a mission, with only one purpose: to forgive him, pray with him, and tell him that despite the abandonment, I still love him and need him to hear it straight from my heart.

The following day we went to the town of Ponce, shared stories, laughed a bit, sat down in the park, and spoke some more. It was at this point when I asked him a direct question. "Why were you never present in my life?" He had no good answer. After more conversations, it became clear that he battled demons his entire life. Demons of alcoholism, self-doubt, and his own trauma he experienced from the abandonment of his own father. He never knew how to be a dad.

During my trip, he asked for forgiveness, and I gave it to him. Was everything restored? No way. We spoke from time to time on the phone after my journey, but that was it. But I believe my journey toward him, and forgiveness extended thereafter, healed something in him, and in me.

When I think of the journey my dad took to encounter his father, I'm incredibly affected. Something was at work in my dad to move him toward someone who wounded him. It certainly took a while to get to this place. But that is natural; forgiveness comes in stages.

THE STAGES OF FORGIVENESS

In many circles of faith, it's commonplace to hear calls for immediate forgiveness. Moments after being wounded, we are taught to offer forgiveness to the offender, regardless of whether it is being requested or not, and sometimes even if it is demanded in manipulative ways. As a result, we say with our mouths what our hearts have not had time to process. This leads to what I call the resentment of forgiveness.

Forgiveness is often a painful, redemptive act, but when done in haste and without careful reflection, it can intensify the rift and resentment we have toward others. Ironically, this kind of forgiveness prolongs the pain because we must concurrently carry the wound and the unprocessed bestowal of grace. Mindless, reactionary acts of forgiveness do not lead to the freedom we long for.

The options before us as people desiring to follow Jesus are not just extending forgiveness or withholding it. The only option is to figure out how to extend it in ways that honor our dignity, attend to our wounds, and reflect the gracious God revealed in his Son. There's a helpful little book that has helped me process this.

Dennis, Sheila, and Matthew Linn co-wrote a book titled *Don't Forgive Too Soon*, which treats forgiveness in similar ways to grief, identifying several stages we must undergo to get to a place of acceptance. In the book, the Linns noted, "When we are hurt, most of us are tempted either to be a passive doormat or to strike back and escalate the cycle of violence." They showed how to forgive in an active, healthy way by moving through a five-step process—framed by the stages of grief coined by Dr. Elisabeth Kübler-Ross—that renounces vengeance and retaliation.[6]

FIVE STAGES IN DYING	FIVE STAGES IN FORGIVENESS
Denial—I don't ever admit I'm dying.	**Denial**—I don't admit I was hurt.
Anger—It's their fault that I'm dying.	**Anger**—It's their fault that I'm hurt.
Bargaining—I set up conditions to be fulfilled before I'm ready to die.	**Bargaining**—I set up conditions before I'm ready to forgive.
Depression—It's my fault that I'm dying.	**Depression**—It's my fault that I'm hurt.
Acceptance—I look forward to death bringing release from the hurt of dying.	**Acceptance**—I look forward to growth from the hurt.

In *stage one,* the denial stage, we know something bad has happened, but we don't admit that it hurt us. We just go on with everyday life. The problem in this stage is that God is locked out because we are not living in reality. And there's only one place where God doesn't dwell: unreality. God dwells only in truth.

In *stage two,* we come to grips with our anger, dwelling on what the other person did to us. This stage is potentially damaging because we can easily fixate on the offense in such a way that we find ourselves in an unending loop.

In *stage three,* we contemplate the possibility that we could forgive, but only if the person does exactly what we want them to (preferably on their knees with our favorite drink from Starbucks). At this stage, the conditions are set but often done so in a way that maintains some level of control.

Stage four brings us to depression. The pain of the offense is so great and the prospects for healing hopeless that we blame ourselves for the predicament we find ourselves in.

Finally, in *stage five,* we accept what happened, recognize that it was in the past, and acknowledge that we have learned from our experience. Acceptance doesn't mean that everything in life has healed, but it does free us from the tyranny of the event and makes it possible for us to move forward.

All these stages are not necessarily linear and neatly lived out, but they offer important language to name the interior movements of the soul. Forgiveness is such a holy, redemptive act that it requires careful attention to the many layers at work within.

ASKING FOR FORGIVENESS

Because of the central themes of the Christian faith (that is, confession, repentance, humility), followers of Christ should be best positioned to model what dispensing forgiveness and requesting forgiveness look like. But we must also address the call to request forgiveness.

The powerful phrase *Will you forgive me?* is one of the most difficult for most of us to utter. I've asked my young children to say these words to each other when they are caught in a skirmish, and through gritted teeth, with their chins plastered to their chests, and eyebrows furrowed, they painfully mumble, "Will you forgive me?" The way it comes out sounds as though they've just had surgery on their jaw.

To request forgiveness can feel like admitting guilt, which is why it's so hard to do. But our world—the personal one filled with friends, family, and co-workers, or the public one that exists outside our little community—cannot move beyond the fractures without getting this right.

Whether we are talking about a child who took another

child's toy, or a nation colonizing another nation's land, we must become fluent in the foreign dialect of forgiveness-asking. I recognize the complex nature of this. For example, there are events that transpire in our lives that are seen from vastly different vantage points. For one person, there was no offense; therefore, there's no forgiveness to request. Yet, for the other person, the wound inflicted was clear as day.

I think of a conversation I had with a relatively new congregant who didn't like what I said one Sunday morning. After a few conversations in which I clarified my theological thought process, the person was still very unhappy with my conclusion. The closing comment from this person was something to the effect of, "It's okay, Pastor Rich. I forgive you." After hearing this, I stared out into space with great puzzlement. I thought to myself, *Why in the world do I need to be forgiven?*

In these moments, by God's grace, we must be able to gain clarity on how the other person has perceived the conflict and with humility name our blind spots and work toward healing. And, unfortunately, our way of asking for forgiveness often leaves much to be desired. In asking for forgiveness, we are to focus on our actions, not the person's perception of the event. For example, to focus on the person's perception leads us to saying things like, "I'm sorry *you* feel that way" or "I'm sorry *you* took offense at what I said." This approach has not and will not heal our relationships.

In the book *A Good Apology,* psychologist Molly Howes explained her four-step model for the powerful yet resisted act of making amends. The approach she offered is worth exploring for a moment. From her experience with many patients on this topic, she came up with four components for doing this well:

1. Listen to and empathize with the other person's hurt.

2. Make a sincere statement of regret and acknowledge harmful actions.

3. Make restitution for the pain caused.

4. Prevent repetition of the injury.[7]

Rather than exploring each of these steps in detail, I want to share how I have attempted to live the ideas out in my marriage. A few years ago, I gathered with thirty other pastors and their spouses for a leadership event. As part of this event, I was asked if I would be interested in writing a letter requesting forgiveness from my wife, Rosie. In addition to writing it, I was also asked to read the letter in front of the sixty people present in the room. Somehow I said yes. Here's the letter I wrote:

Rosangela, my love,
　　As I have been reflecting on our marriage over the past thirteen years, I have been reminded of the various ways I have not been fully present to you in a way that your fears, concerns, and objections have been truly heard by me.
　　Every month, we sit to talk about our calendars. As I share with you about the evening meetings and speaking opportunities that might keep me out

until late at night, I'm aware of the anxiety and desolation that you feel from time to time. I'm also aware that I have pushed forward, minimizing your perspective and nonchalantly justifying why it all can work out just fine.

I've also noticed my irritation when you try to get me to see my personal limits, your limits, and our collective limits as a family. I have often regarded these limits as things to push through, and as a result, you have not truly been heard or seen by me.

I recall you saying things like, "You're going to do what you want to do any way," and as I recall those moments, I find myself deeply saddened by my callousness toward your experience and the current season of life we're in as a family with young kids. I ask for your forgiveness for the ways I have not honored or cherished your perspective, advice, and words of caution.

You have seen time and time again when I have overextended myself and regretted not listening to you. And instead of listening more often, I have continued the pattern of not seeing our family limits as a gift.

In retrospect, reflecting on the moments when you have lovingly expressed the limits of your personal life, my life, or our family life, I have seen that God has been coming through you. In many ways, I'm not just resisting you; I've been resisting God. And time and time again, you gently remind me that I can't do it all.

Knowing that you have felt invisible in moments like these has struck me to the core. On our wedding day, I promised to love you first and foremost, and I'm increasingly aware that I have not loved you well in these moments.

Honey, I ask for your forgiveness for the ways I haven't listened to you.

I ask your forgiveness for the lack of true presence that you deserve in these moments. I ask your forgiveness for the nonchalant ways I have brushed aside significant concerns you have expressed.

I ask your forgiveness and promise to make space in my times with God in prayer to better consider your words and feelings.

Finally, I ask your forgiveness for the ways I haven't better prioritized our own family's calendar, leaving you alone to plan our lives. I promise to be better engaged in the planning of memory-making family moments.

I truly desire that you would feel loved, cherished, and treasured, especially in these kinds of moments.

I love you, honey.

Rich

In our marriage, this calendar issue has been one of the most difficult tensions to manage, which is why I was able to name my faults with specificity. Even so, this letter took several hours to craft. Did it solve everything? No. Have I slipped up again? Sadly, yes. But naming my errors in this way—and requesting forgiveness—has strengthened our marriage in significant ways.

FORGIVENESS AND THE GOSPEL

This chapter would be incomplete without pausing to highlight the gospel and forgiveness. The gospel is absurd to many because of the scandal of God's grace. This is perhaps most prominently demonstrated as Jesus was being crucified. As Jesus was being lynched, the first thing he said was remarkable. He interceded for the angry mob, imploring the Father to forgive them. He cried out, "Father, forgive them, for they do not know what they are doing" (Luke 23:34).

Before he asked for anything for himself, he asked for something for them—and us. This was his primary concern. For us, if we forgive at all, it is distinctly secondary. First, we say, "Let the offender ask for forgiveness and then pardon will be offered." But through the Cross, we see the profundity of God's love.

Jesus on the cross showcased preemptive forgiveness. We are familiar with preemptive war (that is, we are going to strike you before you strike us), but Jesus had this thing he did that shocked people in ancient Israel. He would offer forgiveness to people who weren't looking for it. In one story, a few men brought their paralyzed friend to Jesus. They came with one agenda: physical healing. Yet Jesus's first words to the man were, "Take heart, son; your sins are forgiven" (Matthew 9:2).

If we were on the cross, we might say to those crucifying us, "Your day is coming!" or "What goes around comes around." But look at the Son of God pronouncing grace over a violent, murderous mob.

I heard a story of preacher and theologian Will Willimon talking to a congregant about a distressing situation. She was being abused by her boyfriend. She said to Willimon, "I've prayed to God for the strength to be able to forgive him." He promptly responded, "No. First you tell him that he is wrong, that if he abuses you again, you are going to call the cops, have him thrown in jail, and then, and only then, if he stops, then we'll talk forgiveness."[8] I think that's the proper pastoral response.

I end this chapter with our eyes fixed on Jesus not because this is *exactly* how we are to live this out but because our acts of forgiveness are to flow from the glorious forgiveness exemplified in Jesus. Just look at the Lord on the cross. He prays for forgiveness first. Jesus shows them that his love for us is never conditioned upon our love for him. We tend to believe that God is subject to the vicious ways of humanity. Some of us live in considerable condemnation and fear of his believing that once we mess up, he is going to take out his cosmic belt and whip us. But Jesus teaches us that God's love shatters our limited understanding. In this, Jesus ushers us into a new reality, showing us what God is really like. A story told by Henri Nouwen captures this beautifully:

> An old man . . . used to meditate early every morning under a big tree on the bank of the Ganges. One morning after he had finished his meditation, the old man opened his eyes and saw a scorpion floating helplessly in the water. As the scorpion was washed closer to the tree, the old man quickly stretched himself out on one of the long roots that branched out into the river and reached out to rescue the drowning creature. As soon as he touched it, the scorpion stung him.

Instinctively the man withdrew his hand. A minute later, after he had regained his balance, he stretched himself out again on the roots to save the scorpion. This time the scorpion stung him so badly with its poisonous tail that his hand became swollen and bloody and his face contorted with pain.

At that moment, a passerby saw the old man stretched out on the roots struggling with the scorpion and shouted, "Hey, stupid old man, what's wrong with you? Only a fool would risk his life for the sake of an ugly, evil creature. Don't you know you could kill yourself trying to save that ungrateful scorpion?"

The old man turned his head. Looking into the stranger's eyes he said calmly, "My friend, just because it is the scorpion's nature to sting, that does not change my nature to save."[9]

The world will ultimately become whole through grace. In the meantime, God invites us to anticipate that future by being people rooted in love, through forgiveness. In so doing, we think of the beautiful image of the One who knows our sins and failures and pronounces pardon over us.

Forgiveness ultimately is a revelation of divine love, the kind of love that forms us more deeply than the world's cycle of retribution and violence. It draws us, even in the brokenness of the world, into the kind of strong, loving life that God lives and Christ showed us so clearly.

CHAPTER 9

LOVE IN PUBLIC

Justice in the Way of Jesus

L oving God "first" is not a biblical idea.
(Did that get your attention?)

Let me say more. Somewhere along the line, it became popular to "put God first." This cliché, harmless as it seems, has infiltrated the thinking of countless Christians. That has led to a reduced, compartmentalized idea of love. And like all ideas, it soon begins to shape the practical stuff of life. When most people speak of "keeping God first" or "loving God first," that is an idea that begins abstract but always turns concrete. And however pious the original intention, practically, this sentiment usually results in disconnection from the rest of life.

In the assumptions that are often held in the phrase "Put God first," rather than seeing God's presence in all our encounters, we give what we believe is due to God (verbal/rational/emotional acknowledgment for blessings, and so on), then move on. We feel that our love has been "done" when we say amen or when the last chords have quieted after a powerful worship experience. But God is not to be loved "first"; he is to be loved in and through all. The biblical idea is that we love God by means of all our loves, including those that in fact seem quite down to earth. In fact, to summarize and synthesize many of Christ's most essential teachings, to love our neighbor is to give what's due to God.

But being rooted in love is not to be lived out in our private lives; it's to be demonstrated in the larger, public world we inhabit. That's where we are ending our journey, focusing on how justice forms love for all to see.

This multilayered love is the theological basis for Christian justice. Justice is not something we do after we have "loved God." Justice is one of the primary ways to love him. It is essential, not an extra. This is Christianity 101. The apostle John said it this way: "Whoever does not love their brother and sister, whom they have seen, cannot love God, whom they have not seen" (1 John 4:20). Let the radical nature of that statement sink in. How would we respond if someone came into our church and preached such a message, referencing the precise category of person that you would really like to leave out? What does our response to that question say about our true desire to love God "first"?

The love John speaks of is one built not on sentimentality but in concrete acts of care—care that intersects the true wounds and needs of those around us. The scandal of Christianity is that we love and encounter God through people, especially those on the margins of society, the edges of our awareness, or the "wrong" side of a conflict (an "enemy"). If the love we claim to have doesn't lead to a commitment to seeing wholeness and justice, we will have short-circuited God's love.

Any talk of Christian love that does not faithfully wrestle with the application of it in larger, public matters is a betrayal of faith. To speak meaningfully of love is to care about justice. Professor Cornel West has said it best: "Justice is what love looks like in public." Justice in the way of the Hebrew prophets, the tradition Jesus follows, is an act of profound love. It is the public dimension through which the Shema and the greatest commandment to love God and neighbor are fulfilled. Love must transcend our individual experiences. It must encompass the larger interpersonal and institutional realities we find ourselves in.

The relationship between Christian faith and justice is a long one. Yet in the past century, there have been many who have spoken of justice as if it is a departure from the gospel. Notions of justice—especially "social justice"—have become the line many draw to determine the legitimacy of one's faith. This resistance recalls words from the Black mystic and civil rights leader Howard Thurman, who asked,

> Why is it that Christianity seems impotent to deal radically, and therefore effectively, with the issues of discrimination and injustice on the basis of race, religion, and national origin? Is this impotency due to a betrayal of the genius of the religion, or is it due to a basic weakness in the religion itself?[1]

For Thurman, the Christianity Jesus introduced was one that incorporated the call to justice. It did not espouse impotency nor weakness in this arena. Rather, Christianity found its authority in the ability it has to speak to the real problems and pain of a given society.

When I became a Christian as a nineteen-year-old, I was fixated on one thing: getting people into heaven. I would self-righteously observe neighbors in Brooklyn who committed themselves to local neighborhood initiatives. I would bemoan that they were wasting their energy on a world that would pass away. What mattered was an individual decision for Jesus. Gratefully, what I would come to learn shortly after was that God cared about how my neighborhood—and the whole world—was ordered. Through mentors and good books, I would start to grasp the idea that God was not looking for me to be superspiritual; he was wanting me to firmly place my feet on the ground and see his heart for the gritty everyday existence I lived in.

I would begin to see that Jesus clearly wanted his followers to be more concerned with God's kingdom coming on earth as it is in heaven than with us getting out of earth into heaven. This revelation has only grown over the years.

NO NEUTRAL LOVE

Justice, like many other terms, is a "Rorschach word." The Rorschach test, developed in 1921 by a Swiss psychiatrist, is an ink-blotted image that reveals some level of psychological functioning. Different people look at the same image and come to radically different conclusions about what they are viewing.

Some words, socially speaking, have a similar effect, in that each of us view them differently. The differences inhibit our ability to collaborate in ways that lead to healing. For some people, justice means *my rights and freedom,* whereas for others, it means *socialism.* For some it means *faithfulness to the gospel,* and for others, the *forsaking of the gospel.* When some think about justice, they think in terms of *punishment for crimes committed.* For others, justice is another way of understanding *karma*—that you get what you deserve.

Theologian Scot McKnight wisely contends that the starting point for understanding justice must not begin by looking to the surrounding culture. He wrote,

> But justice for the *Christian* is not about freedom or liberty, rights, individualism, or the pursuit of happiness. When that is what justice means to the Christian, that Christian has adopted Western values as the standard by which justice is defined. Christians can't let the U.S. Constitution (or John Stuart Mill or Karl Marx) define what "justice" means. We have to define justice in a way consistent with what Jesus meant by "kingdom."[2]

The "justice" of Jesus has its roots in the oldest parts of the Bible. Throughout the Old Testament, we learn that God's love is not neutral. God takes sides.

Yes, it is true that God loves everyone. It is also true that he has a track record of paying *particular* attention to those whom society ostracizes or overlooks. Like a parent who tenderly comes to the aid of a sick child in a home with healthy siblings, God comes to the aid of those mistreated. He prioritizes their care and well-being. The God revealed in the story of Israel cannot stomach injustice. Let's look at a few passages and explanations introducing them.

Justice is to be expressed in the fair treatment of all by God's people, regardless of their national or ethnic identity:

Do not deny justice to your poor people in their
lawsuits. Have nothing to do with a false charge
and do not put an innocent or honest person to
death, for I will not acquit the guilty.

Do not accept a bribe, for a bribe blinds those
who see and twists the words of the innocent.
(Exodus 23:6–8)

God cares about those who are disenfranchised or disad-
vantaged:

The LORD works righteousness
and justice for all the oppressed. (Psalm 103:6)

The psalmist promised that God will come to aid those
who cannot protect themselves:

I know that the LORD secures justice for the poor
and upholds the cause of the needy. (Psalm
140:12)

Isaiah noted the way this vulnerable group has been
overlooked and calls the people of God to step in to represent him in society:

Learn to do right; seek justice.
Defend the oppressed.
Take up the cause of the fatherless;
plead the case of the widow. (Isaiah 1:17)

Amos the prophet even went so far as to say (in God's own
voice) that religion without justice is worse than worthless:

I hate, I despise your religious festivals;
    your assemblies are a stench to me.
Even though you bring me burnt offerings and
      grain offerings,
    I will not accept them.
Though you bring choice fellowship offerings,
    I will have no regard for them.
Away with the noise of your songs!
    I will not listen to the music of your harps.
But let justice roll on like a river,
    righteousness like a never-failing stream!
      (Amos 5:21–24)

There's much to draw from just this short list of passages about what justice looks like. (And there are many dozens of other similar passages in the Bible!) Let me synthesize a few ideas to help us better make sense of justice as seen in Scripture, beginning with the truth that justice is primarily about the righteousness of God. In other words, justice is the Lord's.

This is foundational to begin any conversation on the matter. But it's not only something God *does*—it's who he *is*. God *is* just. His very *essence* is characterized by justice. It is inseparable from his love in a fallen world because it is how his love looks when it meets the injustice of sin. His justice is not at odds with his love. It never has been. It could never be. God's love is always just. His justice is always loving. We need not choose between the two. At its core, righteousness is God's never-ending pursuit to right our world. As priest and theologian Fleming Rutledge noted, justice "doesn't refer to a threatening abstract quality that God has over against us. It is much more like a verb than a noun, because it refers *to the power of God to make right what has been wrong.*"[3]

This is made true in Christ. On the cross, sin is judged in the crucified body of Jesus. The dark power that has been at work in the world is placed on Jesus, and in his death and subsequent resurrection, that power is defeated. What is most wrong with the world (sin) is conquered in Christ, and the world is being made right in him. In the Son's crucifixion, God's justice and love was revealed. In this act, God dealt definitively with sin—not winking at it but overpowering it with saving love. Sinners are declared righteous. God has judged sin and justified sinners.

To say that God is righteous is to recognize his commitment to addressing wrongdoing. The task of justice, then, becomes an act of imitation. We work for justice because it's central to who God is.

This truth means that justice, biblically speaking, is definitively more relational than individual. As mentioned earlier, the Western emphasis on our individual rights, albeit important, is not what is stressed in the Bible. You won't find Jesus imploring his disciples to appeal to their "rights." Stay with me here. It's important to say this, because as we explored in the earlier chapters on sin and the possessed powers, something as good as our rights can become twisted, leading to a self-oriented way of being that roots out love.

Freedom can undermine the common good; autonomy can endanger our collective well-being. When this happens, this is no longer biblical justice. Why? Because "a Christian sense of justice is one shaped by the Christian story. And that means a Christian sense of justice is shaped by love of

God and love of others instead of a Western, individualized, and modernist concept of freedom and rights."[4] Justice is the right ordering of relationships. It's an act of organizing life through mutuality and not coercion, humility and not dominance, generosity and not greed, compassion rather than indifference. The challenge, of course, is seeing these elements of justice expressed in our respective contexts, but it's important to situate justice relationally. This brings me to my next observation, which is that biblical justice is relational but is to be carried out systematically.

Throughout Holy Scripture, whenever there is abuse or neglect, God calls for a practical restructuring of concern, as well as the judgment of those in power. Repeatedly, justice is not simply demonstrated through individual acts of mercy. It's carried out by addressing the way power is misused. Mercy means bandaging up people bloodied in life. Justice refers to systemically stopping those who are bloodying up people in the first place, and creating an environment for everyone's flourishing. Christ's followers are called to both kinds of ministries, especially on behalf of the poor and powerless.

Again, biblical justice prioritizes the poor and powerless. You will never read a Bible verse that says, "God is the defender of the rich." It doesn't exist. However, you will find plenty of verses declaring God's deep concern for the poor. This is not to say that God doesn't love those with wealth, but he is overwhelmingly on the side of those suffering from injustice. We should be as well.

To prioritize the poor and powerless is not to agree with every theological conviction that purports to represent them; it means to join our voices to theirs, especially when

they are on the receiving end of mistreatment, whether spiritually, physically, emotionally, or economically. Additionally, to prioritize the poor is to affirm that poverty means
the lack not of competence but of economic capacity. To
join our lives to the poor is to trust that they often know
best what they need and how to climb out of their condition. They need tangible support.

All these observations lead to an overarching truth: Justice is to be aimed at restoration, not simply retribution.

In our culture, the main category for justice is found in
the courtroom. Justice is an act of retribution. It is punishment for wrongdoing. Biblically, there's no denying that
this is a component of justice. There are plenty of Levitical
laws that emphasize judgment for sin. And quite frankly,
most of us are glad for it. When a person is rightly convicted
of murder, the judgment is seen as an act of accountability.

In 2021, when Minnesota police officer Derek Chauvin
was sentenced to twenty-two and a half years in prison,
many Black and Brown people across the United States cel-
ebrated. Yet many of those same people still lamented—not
because they wanted Chauvin to be declared innocent but
because at the end of the day, George Floyd remained dead.
What was done was done. The grief highlighted the deeper
longing for justice we all carry—a justice marked by restoration and healing, not punishment and condemnation.

In recent years, there have been greater calls for restor-
ative justice. Rather than ending one's story in punishment,
this way of thinking calls for accountability, compassion,
self-examination, and a clear process toward personal and
interpersonal healing. When I hear of the efforts being
made in this arena, I can't help but think of the justice of
God.

OBSTACLES TO JUSTICE

Again, justice in the fullest and best sense of the word is about love. But much stands in the way of bringing our lives to this sacred task. The work of justice requires a theological and emotional reimagining. Not all of us are called to the same level of engagement, but we are all commissioned by Christ to serve those around us in concrete ways. Yet, some significant barriers remain, much of them internal.

As a pastor of a diverse group of people who have often had mixed opinions on the centrality of justice to the gospel, I've noticed various points of resistance. For some, the pushback is rooted in meritocracy. A recent story comes to mind.

Meritocracy

In 2020, on the day of Juneteenth—a federal holiday celebrating the end of slavery—there was a collective sense of celebration among Black and Brown people on my social media feed. In the process of the festivities, there were calls for justice and ongoing liberation. It seemed as if everyone went to social media to post an image, reflection, or essay related to an unofficial national holiday at the time. I saw countless White people, as well as Asians and people of Latin descent, share tidbits of Black history. Ordinary people and celebrities alike did this, but one celebrity's post stood out. Donovan Mitchell, the star basketball player for the Utah Jazz, posted an image on Instagram with the words "free•*ish* since 1865." Mitchell was trying to communicate the idea that although slavery ended in 1865, there are still inequities and injustice in our nation.

Well, it didn't take much for the collective gasp of many people—predominantly White males—to surface, followed by mean-spirited, myopic, and mythological words attempting to discredit Mitchell for having the nerve to categorize himself in this manner, being the millionaire he is. Here are some of their comments:

- "You're more free than 99% of us."
- "When you make millions playing basketball but you're only 'freeish.'"
- "Free ish???? Knock it off, you're not a victim of anything. Coming from a millionaire, this is unacceptable."

On and on the comments went until his Instagram trended on Twitter. Apparently, wealth is a superpower that protects Black and Brown people from the forces of racial aggression.

Meritocracy is the belief that individual effort is what is ultimately responsible for one's success, which is a far cry from the truth. If we succeeded, we had help—all of us. Yet the pernicious outworking of this myth is the corresponding belief that any success gained from this effort inoculates us from any claim of injustice. It's the essence of the American Dream with a dash of myopia. When it becomes the lens through which we see the world, it is virtually impossible to live with empathy and recognize the larger, structural realities at work in the world.

This emphasis on meritocracy is a core component of the American value system. It presupposes that experiences of injustice are usually tied to lack of effort. I've heard this repeated from many, from upwardly mobile White people to successful Asian immigrants to highly educated Latinos:

- "If these people only worked harder, they would not be poor."
- "If they pursued an education, they would live in greater freedom."
- "If they didn't rely on the government, they would experience success."

It's ironic that Christians who believe in salvation by grace and not our merit can be so formed by a social theology of meritocracy. But, clearly, no amount of money or success—especially for people of color—can be a protective coating against unfair treatment in this world. Just ask Oprah Winfrey about an experience she had in Zurich, Switzerland, where a shop assistant refused to show her a handbag because it was "too expensive." Ask the Black Harvard-educated tennis player James Blake about an encounter in New York City, where he was attacked and slammed to the ground and handcuffed by several White plainclothes police officers.[5] Or recall the story of Harvard professor Henry Louis Gates, Jr., who was arrested at his own home by an officer investigating a report of a robbery.[6] Meritocracy is a myth and must be resisted for the sake of love.

Me-Oriented Catharsis

Another obstacle that stands in the way of justice is the pseudo-justice mentality that is daily prevalent on social media. I'm often guilty of having this myself. Much of what passes for justice is simply outrage baptized in disembodied calls for fairness. But diagnosis is not justice. Naming the problems is not justice. It might be the start of justice, but it can never be the end.

We have become adept at naming problems without pursuing solutions. It's common for many to deride what seems like unjust policies, only to order stuff from Amazon five minutes later. The injustice we renounce has a way of sneaking through the back door of our psyches. This is why renouncing must be tempered with great humility.

Justice must move beyond emotional catharsis toward a commitment to action in some capacity. Outrage is a great brand builder but a poor justice maker.

Theological Sidestepping

The work of justice is hindered by endless theologizing. Theologian James Cone painted a poignant picture of this. In the 1960s, he wrote, "While churches are debating whether a whale swallowed Jonah, the state is enacting inhuman laws against the oppressed."[7] It's a vivid image. Much of the resistance around justice is done in the name of the Bible. Whether it's Christians spending inordinate amounts of time on minor theological points or using the Bible to critique calls for justice, injustice persists because we have made an idol out of orthodoxy. So-called right thinking too often gets in the way of right action. It's the kind of meticulous religiosity that angered Jesus.

In Luke's gospel, he said, "Woe to you Pharisees, because you give God a tenth of your mint, rue and all other kinds of garden herbs, but you neglect justice and the love of God. You should have practiced the latter without leaving the former undone" (11:42).

Jesus was essentially saying that theological correctness that impedes justice positions us for judgment.

THE OVERWHELMING BURDEN OF JUSTICE

At the height of the global pandemic, *The New York Times* published a story about the severe economic impact that immigrants suffered. One heartbreaking story, about a thirty-one-year-old Mexican woman in Queens, explained how "she keeps her money in cash, after closing her bank account because she couldn't pay the service fees. She never touches the last $20 bill beneath her mattress, she said, saving it for an emergency taxi ride should something go wrong."[8] Unspeakably, she has had to survive on a hundred dollars a week, living in a cramped room, after spending six months in a shelter.

A gesture from her eleven-year-old son, Christopher, captured the enormity of the situation. He cut a hole out of the side of a box, making it into an ATM. With slips of paper made to look like money, he asked, "Mami, do you need money?" as he offered his mother one hundred dollars. Thankfully, this Queens family has been able to take advantage of government and community resources, but I can't help but think about the gesture of her son. When I look at the immense problems of the world, sometimes I feel like I'm offering a hundred dollars of imagined money to help a world burdened by crushing need.

Yet I'm reminded of an important truth: We are not called to fix the world but to faithfully respond with the resources, strength, and love we have. Even so, the pain of the world can be quite overwhelming. The apparent insignificance of our actions can feel like a drop in the ocean.

While all this might be true, the call to justice is not about fruitfulness but faithfulness. It is in the especially trying times that Jesus's words about the kingdom of God being a mustard seed are needed (see Matthew 13:31–32). In God's way of doing things, the small, hidden, incremental acts of love have a way of being harnessed by the Spirit for great good. This is the way of the Cross.

It's possible to have a life that doesn't appear fruitful to the world but is faithful to God. The Cross looks like failure but is the greatest act of faithfulness, which has led to incalculable fruitfulness. I often wonder how much of a difference I'm making helping the world to becoming more just. It all seems so overwhelming to comprehend. But the Holy Spirit reminds me that discipleship is not about fruitfulness but faithfulness. My task is to be faithful. God will take care of the fruit. At the end of it all, Jesus will not say, "Well done, good and successful servant" or "Well done, good and influential servant" or "Well done, good and high-capacity servant," but rather, "Well done, good and faithful servant!" (Matthew 25:21).

PRACTICING JUSTICE

For the rest of this chapter, I want to broaden the idea of practicing justice in whatever context we find ourselves in. If justice is to be an act of love, it demands something from us: our dignifying attention, a local focus, and a countercultural community.

Our Dignifying Attention

By dignifying attention, I have in mind the act of viewing others with a loving gaze. Justice in the way of Jesus is not

simply about policies driven by power but also a reordering
of social life fueled by love. This kind of love requires our
attention. The healing story in Acts 3 comes to mind.

As Peter and John were on their way to worship, they
encountered a lame man who was put in front of the temple
to beg every day. As the newly Holy Spirit–empowered disciples were about to walk in, they fixed their attention on
the man. They didn't flippantly throw change at him but
spoke words that are the hallmark of justice. The passage
notes that "Peter looked straight at him, as did John. Then
Peter said, 'Look at us!'" (verse 4). Justice in the way of
Jesus takes the time to look at people, dignifying them with
our attention. I think of all the times I've done the exact
opposite.

Recently, as my twelve-year-old daughter, Karis, and I
were returning home from her gymnastics class, we hit
some traffic on Queens Boulevard. As we inched our way
through rush-hour traffic, a woman approached my car
with a clear plastic bag of mangoes in her hand. The jam-
packed boulevard was her office. As she neared me, I inched
up, averting her eyes.

As my car slowly moved forward, I peeked at the side-
view mirror to see her approaching the car behind me.
That's when Karis, in tears, shouted, "How could you do
that? She needs the money. How could you ignore her like
that?" In shock, I began to defend myself: "Karis, I don't
have any cash on me. I can't buy stuff from everyone selling
things in the street." She crossed her arms, and tears
streamed down her face. I knew I had missed it.

Like Peter and John, I didn't have silver or gold in my
pocket, nor did I have dollars or cents. But I missed out on

the currency that brings healing, even in a small way: the currency of loving attentiveness. Justice requires us to attend to people, to see them, to truly recognize their presence. It's the refusal to depersonalize people into mirages.

In Ralph Ellison's classic novel *Invisible Man,* he captured the burden of invisibility. He wrote the book in the 1950s, in a time of overt racial injustice. He noted that what made the experience of being Black back then so difficult wasn't simply the hostility that Black men and women encountered; it was the invisibility that characterized everyday life for them. Ellison painfully captured the experience:

> I am an invisible man. No, I am not a spook like those who haunted Edgar Allen Poe; nor am I one of your Hollywood-movie ectoplasms. I am a man of substance, of flesh and bone, fiber and liquids—and I might even be said to possess a mind. I am invisible, understand, simply because people refuse to see me.[9]

Our Local Focus

In Dostoyevsky's novel *The Brothers Karamazov,* Zosima, the elderly monk, offered a clarifying word on the demanding nature of love. He said, "Love in action is a harsh and dreadful thing compared with love in dreams."[10] It's easy to love in our dreams, to idealize and romanticize love. But, ultimately, love in dreams is not love at all. Love requires our action. This is important for people who are deluded into believing that love and justice can be delivered behind our keyboards and smartphones. Love in action requires . . . action. This is core to our work for justice.

Justice necessitates engagement. *Local* engagement.

Whether we are talking about petitioning community leadership to add a stop sign at a busy street, organizing public-safety measures with neighbors, or training teenagers to be community organizers, justice is often best done in the immediate communities we occupy. Again, Christian justice is about ordering relationships to be marked by love expressed in individual, interpersonal, and institutional environments.

When I consider New Life Fellowship, I'm blown away by the diversity of justice initiatives carried out by followers of Christ. I've seen congregational leaders with our community-development corporation partner with other churches in Queens to advocate for affordable housing. I've witnessed the great work happening through our church's Young Governors program, where dozens of teens have been trained to effectively identify and creatively respond to needs in the neighborhood. I've watched as anti-poverty empowerment programs were started to lift low-income families out of perpetual struggle.

Whether our justice work is flowing from the life of a congregation, through one's participation in the local community board, or at the food pantry, we are called to put flesh on our theology.

A Countercultural Community

American theologian Stanley Hauerwas has said, "The task of the church is to serve as the best example of what God can do with human community."[11] I couldn't agree more. The church as a whole, and the local church in part, has the holy task of establishing a colony of heaven here on earth. When people step into our buildings, homes, and fellowships, they are to be exposed to an otherworldly community—a community not formed by antagonisms but by grace, not by gossip but by honor, not by selfishness but by generosity. The church is the best place for justice to be worked out. In forming communities marked by justice, we offer a sneak peek as to what the world will look like when Christ fully reigns. Because we are people endowed with the Holy Spirit, God's life is shed upon our hearts to show the world the future that awaits. This is the compelling story of the first Christians in the book of Acts:

> They devoted themselves to the apostles' teaching and to fellowship, to the breaking of bread and to prayer. Everyone was filled with awe at the many wonders and signs performed by the apostles. All the believers were together and had everything in common. They sold property and possessions to give to anyone who had need. Every day they continued to meet together in the temple courts. They broke bread in their homes and ate together with glad and sincere hearts, praising God and enjoying the favor of all the people. And the Lord added to their number daily those who were being saved. (2:42–47)

Read these words again. This is a community marked by justice—not the justice of individualism and personal rights, but one marked by compassion, generosity, and wholeness. They share meals with glad hearts and have obtained favor with the watching world. The early church would go on to experience division and pain, like every other human community, but this gives us a vision of what God wants to do through us.

As the leader of our community in Queens, I'm constantly thinking about this Acts passage. I'm aware of people within our church family who are struggling financially and have little to no opportunities for respite. I continue to reflect on the practical ways we can care for one another in our need. This is a lifelong work, and the church is tasked with carrying it out.

THE JUSTIFIED CARRYING OUT JUSTICE

I end this chapter with a word of warning and a word of hope. First, the warning. Working for justice can become a way to justify ourselves before God. If we are not careful, the good work we give ourselves to can become another idol that takes the rightful place of Jesus. We must be on guard against the temptation to establish an identity outside of the love of God in Christ.

If we don't live from the center of God's love, working for justice can be just another creative way to meet the unrelenting needs of our egos. When that happens, the work for justice is no longer about the poor and mistreated but about our own unmet needs.

We work for justice not because it justifies us; rather, because we've been justified, we work for justice.

We are called to work with urgency, knowing that the needs are great, and also with patience, convinced that God is near. We pour ourselves out in love because this is how Christ longs to live through us, but we recognize our limitations. We seek the peace of our cities and towns because we are called to be salt and light, and we confess that only Jesus will make all things new.

To have a good, beautiful, and kind life—one formed by

love—requires us to extend our faith beyond the borders of our private emotional and spiritual concerns. We are called into a larger story, one characterized by participation in God's kingdom. It's the kind of participation that drives out passivity.

When Jesus taught his disciples to pray, he instructed them to say, "Your kingdom come, your will be done, on earth as it is in heaven" (Matthew 6:10). Is that not love? Is that not justice? To pray these words is not to passively say, "Lord, there's nothing we can do, so please fix this world."

Rather, the Lord's Prayer calls us to say, "Lord, there's so *much* we can do, but only ever in your power."

Can I get an amen?

AFTERWORD

If we want to live in love, we must recognize that we already exist in it. This paradox is one of the deep truths I learned from Ruth Burrows, a modern-day Carmelite nun. Burrows wrote,

> A baby in its mother's womb is in a relationship with her but is unaware of it and does not respond to the mother's intense love and desire to give herself to the child. The relationship with God on the human side can remain as minimal as that of the baby.[1]

What a profound image! As a baby exists in its mother's womb, we exist in the "womb" of God. We are already *in* love. We exist inside of it. What, after all, could exist apart from the grace and sustaining power of our beloved, loving Creator?

Throughout our journey together, we have named the "worms" fragmenting our lives and relationships. We have looked at the forces that keep us from living lives that are good, beautiful, and kind. If I could sum up everything I've written thus far, there's one word that would suffice: *abide*.

To abide in God's love can sound ethereal and abstract, like something restricted for the spiritual elite. But it's not. Not at all. Abiding in love is for anyone who wants to do it. But it requires something of most of us: a fundamental shift in our perspective. Many people find it difficult to open themselves to God's love because the image they have of him is not compatible with such love. He is often perceived as the Disappointed One, the Angry One, or the Indifferent One. When one of these false images is in our minds, it makes little sense to open ourselves up to this God.

That is why the fundamental task of living in love and pouring it out on others is found in the healing of our image of God—something Jesus came to do. And as this book ends, along with the journey we've taken together in it, I want to challenge you to begin your next phase of spiritual life with one simple and life-changing challenge. It has two parts: First, I want you to release any image of God that is anything less than pure, self-giving, abundant love. Second, choose—whether you understand it or not—to abide in that love. To dwell in it. To live in it.

You see, in Jesus, we discover the cruciform love of God—the self-giving love that stretches out to us, inviting us into his eternal embrace. His is the love that redeems us. His is the love that forms us to become the embodiment of wholeness for a world tragically fractured and breaking apart more every day.

Opening ourselves to God's love doesn't just absolve us from guilt and shame; it transforms us *into* love. Abiding in his love is the greatest task of life.

Author and speaker Brennan Manning said, "My deepest awareness of myself is that I am deeply loved by Jesus Christ and I have done nothing to earn it or deserve it."[2] I couldn't agree more. To live from this place is the starting point for the transformation of our lives and the world.

In opening ourselves to God's great love, we find the source of our wholeness—the kind of wholeness that mends our fragmented lives.

My prayer for you is that every day you can grow in the depth, breadth, length, and height of this abiding love, because as we do so, imperfect though we may still be, we will find the life of Jesus. And amid this fracturing world, we will find ourselves—slowly, patiently—growing.

Growing good.

Growing beautiful.

Growing kind.

A GUIDE FOR REFLECTION
AND DISCUSSION

INTRODUCTION

Forming Connection

What hopes do you have as you explore this material with others or individually? Take a look at this book's contents page. What do you most look forward to discussing? Why?

Bible Study: 1 Corinthians 12

- Read the text. Which words and phrases stand out to you?
- How do you understand the concept of wholeness? What do you think are the marks of it in a person's life?
- A core part of this book is the call to love well. In your own words, what does it mean to love well?
- At this stage in your life, what would you say are the biggest obstacles to your loving well?

Personal Reflection

In light of this passage, what do you sense is God's invitation to you today?

Taking the Next Step

- Underline and share the words and phrases that are most relevant to you and your story.
- What "worms" are eating away at our society? What are the "worms" eating away at your personal life?
- What would it look like to begin addressing them?

CHAPTER 1: A FAILURE TO LOVE

Forming Connection

Take two minutes to write down your definition of love. In what ways (if any) has your definition of love changed over the years?

Bible Study: Matthew 22:37–40; 1 John 4:11–21; Genesis 3; 4:1–16; 11:1–9

- Read the text. Which words and phrases stand out to you?
- In Matthew 22 and 1 John 4, the measure of love for God is measured by love for a brother or sister. How does this challenge your understanding of how love for God is measured?
- When you read—in the opening stories of Genesis— the ways sin has fractured the world (Adam and Eve's

grasping, Cain's envy, the exclusionism of the Tower of Babel), where do you recognize your own brokenness in these stories?

Personal Reflection

What practical changes might God be inviting you to make in light of 1 John 4:11–21?

Taking the Next Step

- If love is the greatest command, the greatest sin must be failure to love. What connections do you recognize between sin and love in your own spiritual life?
- Confession is one of the most important practices for "uncurving" ourselves. To what degree has this practice shaped your life? How could you incorporate confession (toward God and another person) as a regular spiritual practice?

CHAPTER 2: THE UNSEEN ENEMY

Forming Connection

Some people have a fascination with theology, movies, or books that address ghosts, demons, or unseen forces. Others avoid these things altogether. Where do you fall on that spectrum? Why?

Bible Study: Ephesians 6:13–17

- Read the text. Which words and phrases stand out to you?

- When you think about your own spiritual journey, how much space have you given to the presence of powers and principalities?
- Which parts of the armor of God are you most drawn to? Why?
- Paul says, "Our struggle is not against flesh and blood" (Ephesians 6:12). What changes in our world might become possible if we truly believed this? What might change in your life if you lived as if this were true?

Personal Reflection

What do you sense God inviting you to today in light of this passage?

Taking the Next Step

- The powers seek to depersonalize, deceive, and divide. Which of these three actions are you most inclined to have shape your life? What would it look like for you to do the opposite?
- If you can, describe a time you resisted the ways of the powers in order to follow in the way of Jesus.

CHAPTER 3: HINDERING WOUNDS, HOLY WOUNDS

Forming Connection

To what degree has the idea of trauma played a role in the way you understand yourself?

Bible Study: John 20:24–29

- Read the text. Which words and phrases stand out to you?
- It is noteworthy that the resurrected Jesus still bears the marks of his traumatizing crucifixion on his body. What significance do you draw from this for your own life?
- Jesus shows his wounds to his friends but not to the world at large. What relationship principles can you draw from this?
- Jesus invites Thomas to touch his wounds. It's a vulnerable act. On a scale of 1 to 10, how does vulnerability factor into your relationships with others (1 means not at all; 10 means it's an important part)?

Personal Reflection
What do you sense God inviting you to today in light of this passage?

Taking the Next Step

- Is there a story of personal trauma, perhaps one that you haven't previously categorized as such, that you feel safe enough to share in this group? How does identifying this event as traumatic affect the way you see yourself or the way you see others?
- How could understanding the stories inside us (our woundedness) create stronger bonds of connection between ourselves and others?

- Do you find it difficult to integrate your body with your spirituality? Why or why not?

CHAPTER 4: THE PROBLEM OF PRAYER

Forming Connection

How would you describe your prayer life? What role has silence (specifically during prayer) played on your journey?

Bible Study: John 15:1-8

- Read the text. Which words and phrases stand out to you?
- In this Scripture passage, Jesus is calling his disciples to remain, or abide, in him. What significance do these words hold for you when it comes to prayer?
- What kind of fruit is Christ looking to form in his twelve disciples in this passage? What kind of fruit do you believe God wants to form in you?

Personal Reflection

What do you sense God inviting you to today in light of this passage?

Taking the Next Step

- Contemplative prayer aids us in facing our false self, being an unanxious presence, and stewarding our words. Which of these three fruits of contemplative prayer calls out to you today? Why?

- After reading this chapter, how do you think contemplative prayer can help you address the deep problems of our world?

CHAPTER 5: BEYOND THE WALLS
OF THE FALSE SELF

Forming Connection

How do you define humility? In what situations do you most often find it hard to be humble?

Bible Study: Philippians 2:1–11

- Read the text. Which words and phrases stand out to you?
- What might have been happening in this church community to compel Paul to write these words to the Philippians?
- In this chapter, Paul calls us to imitate the humility of Jesus. What makes Jesus's humility so countercultural?
- As followers of Christ, we are called to value others above ourselves (see verse 3). How difficult do you find it to obey this teaching? Why?
- Paul notes that the humility of Jesus resulted in his death. If you can, describe a time when being humble led to a kind of "death" for you.

Personal Reflection

What do you sense God inviting you to today in light of this passage?

Taking the Next Step

- Cultivating humility means we have nothing to protect, prove, or possess. Which of these three inclinations do you have the most difficulty letting go of? Why?
- As you consider the story of Naaman in this chapter, where does his story connect to yours? What might it look like for you to take off the armor?
- Very few people enjoy receiving correction. What's the internalized message you tell yourself when you are corrected? What thought might God want to replace that message with?

CHAPTER 6: RESISTING REACTIVITY

Forming Connection

What situations make you most anxious? Tell about a time you refused to allow anxiety to keep you from doing something.

Bible Study: Mark 4:35–41

- Read the text. Which words and phrases stand out to you?
- What symptoms of anxiety do you see in this story?
- What connection might Jesus be making between faith and peace?
- What "waves" of anxiety have overflowed into your "boat" in recent days?

Personal Reflection

What do you sense God inviting you to today in light of this passage?

Taking the Next Step

- Anxiety about our automatic reactions to real or perceived threats often leads us to cutting off or being enmeshed. When anxiety emerges within you, in which of the two directions do you tend to go? What does it look like when that happens?
- Self-differentiation is about remaining close to and curious about God, others, and ourselves, especially in times of high anxiety. Think of a story about when you were able to do this successfully. If you don't have one, why do you think self-differentiation hasn't happened for you yet?
- Three practices for cultivating calm presence are emotional self-regulation, naming the messages, and speaking clearly. Which of these three do you need to prioritize in this season of your life? Why?

CHAPTER 7: A BRIDGE, NOT A BARRIER

Forming Connection

How did the family in which you grew up handle conflict? How does this approach shape your current relationships?

Bible Study: Galatians 2:11–21

- Read the text. Which words and phrases from this story stand out to you?
- Review the context provided on pages 142–145 regarding the situation in Galatians.
- What might have become of the church if Paul hadn't confronted Peter on his hypocrisy?
- What significance do you find in the presence of conflict in the Bible?

Personal Reflection

What do you sense God inviting you to today in light of this passage?

Taking the Next Step

- The three stages of relationships can be described as heavenly, hellish, and holding the tensions. When have you allowed yourself to experience all three in a single relationship?
- In this chapter, we see that healthy conflict is disrupted because of triangulation. How often do you find yourself "triangling" others into your conflicts? Why do you think this happens?
- Take a look at the steps to a "clean fight" in this chapter. Think of a current conflict you might be going through. Spend seven to ten minutes to respond in writing to the four steps. If you feel comfortable, share with the group what you've written.

CHAPTER 8: THE GIFT OF FORGIVENESS

Forming Connection

Which do you have more difficulty doing: asking for forgiveness or extending it? Why?

Bible Study: Matthew 18:21–35

- Read the text. Which words and phrases stand out to you?
- When you read Jesus's words about forgiving seventy-seven times, how do you feel?
- How could it be possible that the forgiven person treated his fellow servant harshly even after being forgiven?
- How often do you think about the forgiveness of God in your life? What difference has this made?

Personal Reflection

What do you sense God inviting you to today in light of this passage?

Taking the Next Step

- It's possible to be forgiven yet still live behind the prison bars of unforgiveness. When have you personally observed this to be true?
- Which of these four statements most challenges your thinking about forgiveness?
  - Forgiveness doesn't mean forgetting.

- Forgiveness doesn't mean there are no consequences.
- Forgiveness doesn't mean you no longer feel
  the pain of grieving.
- Forgiveness doesn't always mean reconciliation
  with another person.
- To whom might God be calling you to extend forgiveness? Review the five stages in forgiveness on page
  172, from the book *Don't Forgive Too Soon.* What
  stage might you be in at the moment?

CHAPTER 9: LOVE IN PUBLIC

Forming Connection
What injustices in the world cause the greatest grief and
anger in your life?

Bible Study: Amos 5:21–24

- Read the text. Which words and phrases stand out to
  you?
- If you translated these verses into contemporary language, what would this passage sound like? Take five
  minutes to write it out.
- What spiritual implications can we draw from the Lord
  saying (through Amos) that he has no regard for various offerings when injustice persists?

Personal Reflection
What do you sense God inviting you to today in light of this
passage?

Taking the Next Step

- What role has justice played in your following of Jesus? Why do you think this is so?
- Meritocracy often plays a role in keeping people from pursuing justice. How does this idea influence you and the way you respond to inequities in the world?
- This chapter offers three calls to practicing justice: our dignifying attention, a local focus, and a countercultural community. Which of these do you think you must prioritize in this season of your life? How will that look in action?

ACKNOWLEDGMENTS

It takes a village to write a book. While it's impossible to write a comprehensive list of all who have asked good questions plus offered timely encouragement and gentle but wise pushback, I do want to highlight a few friends on the journey.

Many thanks to my agent, Alex Field. Your calm presence and eager assistance through all the minutia of book writing has been a great gift. I also have so much gratitude for my editor, Paul Pastor. When I articulated the original idea for this book, Paul (ever so gently) would task me with going deeper. *What is the larger, more urgent issue that needs addressing? Where do I want to lead my readers?* These questions—frustrating as it felt in the moment—were so important in helping me gain clarity. It's been a joy to have you as a primary conversation partner, Paul! Many thanks as well to the WaterBrook team. Thank you for your energy and support.

Major thanks to my fellow Puerto Rican Brooklynite, Arnaldo Santiago, for reading everything I sent your way and for your incisive reflections. Your friendship has made me a better writer. My sister, Melissa, also read so much of my early drafts. Thank you for responding to all my texts asking "Have you read it yet?" I'm so grateful for you, sister.

Much of the content in this book flows out of my life in the New Life Fellowship community I have the privilege of pastoring. Many thanks to the board of elders, staff team (special shout-out to Pastor Cate Song), and the dear friends I have the joy of worshipping with. I wrote this book primarily for our community. Thank you for being a good and beautiful and kind church.

I'm so grateful for my two children, Karis and Nathan. Thank you for your words of encouragement as I wrote this book and for the hilarious ways you make fun of me at the dinner table. Daddy loves you.

Finally, my profound gratitude is extended to my wife, Rosie. Thank you for your steady encouragement and prophetic feedback. You have an amazing way of holding these realities together. This book would not be possible without your steadfast support. I love you, darling.

NOTES

INTRODUCTION

1. Langston Hughes, *The Collected Poems of Langston Hughes,* ed. Arnold Rampersad (New York: Vintage, 1995), 135. I recommend you read this brilliant poem in its entirety.

CHAPTER 1: A FAILURE TO LOVE

1. For a full exploration of *incurvatus in se* in the works of Saint Augustine, Martin Luther, and Karl Barth, see Matt Jenson, *The Gravity of Sin: Augustine, Luther, and Barth* on homo incurvatus in se (London: T&T Clark, 2007).

2. "Question 1," Westminster Short Catechism Project, www.shortercatechism.com/resources/wsc/wsc_001.html.

3. Barbara Brown Taylor, *Speaking of Sin: The Lost Language of Salvation* (Lanham, Md.: Cowley, 2001), 4.

4. Thomas Merton, *New Seeds of Contemplation* (Boston: Shambhala, 1961), 94–95.

5. Edwin H. Friedman, *A Failure of Nerve, Revised Edition: Leadership in the Age of the Quick Fix* (New York: Church Publishing, 2017), 58.

6. Karl Barth, *Church Dogmatics: The Doctrine of Reconciliation,* trans. G. W. Bromiley, eds. G. W. Bromiley and T. F. Torrance (New York: T&T Clark International, 2004), 144.

7. Taylor, *Speaking of Sin,* 47, emphasis added.

CHAPTER 2: THE UNSEEN ENEMY

1. Wade Goodwyn, "Waco Recalls a 90-Year-Old 'Horror,'" NPR, May 13, 2006, https://www.npr.org/templates/story/story.php?storyId=5401868.

2. James H. Cone, *The Cross and the Lynching Tree* (Maryknoll, N.Y.: Orbis Books, 2011), xiv.

3. Walter Wink, *Unmasking the Powers: The Invisible Forces That Determine Human Existence* (Philadelphia, Pa.: Fortress, 1986), 41.

4. Hendrik Berkhof, *Christ and the Powers,* trans. John H. Yoder (Scottdale, Pa.: Herald, 1977), 29.

5. James H. Cone, *A Black Theology of Liberation* (Maryknoll, N.Y.: Orbis Books, 2010), 33.

6. C. S. Lewis, *The Screwtape Letters* (New York: HarperOne, 2001), ix.

7. Eldon L. Ham, "The Immaculate Deception: How the Holy Grail of Protectionism Led to the Great Steroid Era," *Marquette Sports Law Review* 19, no. 1 (Fall 2008): 212, emphasis added, https://scholarship.law.marquette.edu/cgi/viewcontent.cgi?article=1027&context=sportslaw.

8. David E. Fitch, *The Church of Us vs. Them: Freedom from a Faith That Feeds on Making Enemies* (Grand Rapids, Mich.: Brazos, 2019), 28.

9. Reinhold Niebuhr, *Moral Man and Immoral Society: A Study in Ethics and Politics* (Louisville, Ky.: Westminster John Knox, 2021).

10. Martin Luther King, Jr., *A Testament of Hope: The Essential Writings and Speeches,* ed. James Melvin Washington (New York: HarperCollins, 1991), 250.

11. Sherry Turkle, *Alone Together: Why We Expect More from Technology and Less from Each Other* (New York: Basic Books, 2011), 243.

12. Marva J. Dawn, *Powers, Weakness, and the Tabernacling of God* (Grand Rapids, Mich.: Eerdmans, 2001), 149.

13. Peter Storey, in Donald B. Kraybill and Linda Gehman Peachey, eds., *Where Was God on September 11? Seeds of Faith and Hope* (Scottdale, Pa.: Herald, 2002).

CHAPTER 3: HINDERING WOUNDS, HOLY WOUNDS

1. Bessel van der Kolk, *The Body Keeps the Score: Brain, Mind, and Body in the Healing of Trauma* (New York: Penguin Books, 2015), 1.

2. Barna Group, *Trauma in America: Understanding How People Face Hardships and the Church Offers Hope* (New York: American Bible Society, 2020), 25.

3. Parker J. Palmer, *A Hidden Wholeness: The Journey Toward an Undivided Life* (San Francisco: Jossey-Bass, 2009), 123.

4. *Merriam-Webster*, s.v. "trauma," www.merriam-webster.com/dictionary/trauma?utm_campaign=sd&utm_medium=serp&utm_source=jsonld.

5. Resmaa Menakem, *My Grandmother's Hands: Racialized Trauma and the Pathway to Mending Our Hearts and Bodies* (Las Vegas: Central Recovery, 2017), 8.

6. Sheila Wise Rowe, *Healing Racial Trauma: The Road to Resilience* (Downers Grove, Ill.: InterVarsity, 2020), 10.

7. Rowe, *Healing Racial Trauma*, 10.

8. Robert Stolorow, *Trauma and Human Existence: Autobiographical, Psychoanalytic, and Philosophical Reflections* (New York: Routledge, 2007), 10, quoted in Rich Villodas, *The Deeply Formed Life: Five Transformative Values to Root Us in the Way of Jesus* (Colorado Springs, Colo.: WaterBrook, 2020), 113–14.

9. Gabor Maté, *When the Body Says No: Exploring the Stress-Disease Connection* (Hoboken, N.J.: Wiley, 2011), 203.

10. Brené Brown, *Dare to Lead: Brave Work, Tough Conversations, Whole Hearts* (New York: Random House, 2018), 166.

11. Curt Thompson, *Anatomy of the Soul: Surprising Connections between Neuroscience and Spiritual Practices That Can Transform Your Life and Relationships* (Carol Stream, Ill.: Tyndale, 2010), 118.

12. Van der Kolk, *Body Keeps the Score*, 13.

13. Stolorow, *Trauma and Human Existence*, 10.

14. Shelly Rambo, *Resurrecting Wounds: Living in the Afterlife of Trauma* (Waco, Tex.: Baylor University, 2017), 4.

15. Rambo, *Resurrecting Wounds*, 145.

CHAPTER 4: THE PROBLEM OF PRAYER

1. Although public prayer undoubtedly has its benefits, remember that when we did have prayer in school (before public school prayer was banned in 1962 in the United States), we still had plenty of social problems, segregation, and racism among them.

2. Saint Augustine, *Confessions: A New Translation by Sarah Ruden* (New York: Modern Library, 2018), 63.

3. John H. Coe and Kyle C. Strobel, eds., *Embracing Contemplation: Reclaiming a Christian Spiritual Practice* (Downers Grove, Ill.: InterVarsity, 2019), 35.

4. Karl Rahner, "Christian Living Formerly and Today," *Theological Investigations VII*, trans. David Bourke (New York: Herder and Herder, 1971), 15.

5. "1987 PDFA Anti-Drug Commercial (This Is Your Brain on Drugs),"

streamed on July 14, 2011, YouTube video, 0:14, posted by "K.J. Norman," www.youtube.com/watch?v=F0kCYP_iPtg.

6. Andrew Newberg and Mark Robert Waldman, *How God Changes Your Brain: Breakthrough Findings from a Leading Neuroscientist* (New York: Ballantine Books, 2010), 7.

7. Benedicta Ward, ed. and trans., *The Desert Fathers: Sayings of the Early Christian Monks* (New York: Penguin Books, 2003), 20.

8. Ward, *Desert Fathers,* 98.

9. Internet Live Stats, www.internetlivestats.com.

10. Douglas Steere, quoted in *Thomas Merton: Contemplative Prayer* (New York: Doubleday, 1996), 12.

CHAPTER 5: BEYOND THE WALLS OF THE FALSE SELF

1. Thomas Merton, *New Seeds of Contemplation* (Boston: Shambhala, 1961), 36.

2. M. Robert Mulholland, Jr., *The Deeper Journey: The Spirituality of Discovering Your True Self* (Downers Grove, Ill.: InterVarsity, 2016), 24.

3. Richard Rohr, quoted in Alice Fryling, *Mirror for the Soul: A Christian Guide to the Enneagram* (Downers Grove, Ill.: InterVarsity, 2017), 10.

4. John Sanidopoulos, "Life and Sayings of Holy Abba John the Dwarf," *Orthodox Christianity Then and Now* (blog), November 9, 2016, www .johnsanidopoulos.com/2010/11/saint-john-dwarf-kolovos.html.

5. Dallas Willard, quoted in John Ortberg, *Soul Keeping: Caring for the Most Important Part of You* (Grand Rapids, Mich.: Zondervan, 2014), 22.

CHAPTER 6: RESISTING REACTIVITY

1. Murray Bowen, quoted in Ronald W. Richardson, *Becoming a Healthier Pastor: Family Systems Theory and the Pastor's Own Family* (Minneapolis, Minn.: Fortress, 2005), 18.

2. Ronald W. Richardson, *Becoming a Healthier Pastor,* 18.

3. Peter L. Steinke, *Congregational Leadership in Anxious Times: Being Calm and Courageous No Matter What* (Lanham, Md.: Rowman & Littlefield, 2006), 45.

CHAPTER 7: A BRIDGE, NOT A BARRIER

1. Dietrich Bonhoeffer, *Life Together,* Dietrich Bonhoeffer Works—Reader's Edition, ed. Victoria J. Barnett, trans. Daniel W. Bloesch (Minneapolis, Minn.: Fortress, 2015), 10.

2. Sherry Turkle, *Reclaiming Conversation: The Power of Talk in a Digital Age* (New York: Penguin, 2015), 29.

3. Turkle, *Reclaiming Conversation,* 28.

4. Curt Thompson, *The Soul of Shame: Retelling the Stories We Believe About Ourselves* (Downers Grove, Ill.: InterVarsity, 2015), 25.

5. Edwin H. Friedman, *Generation to Generation: Family Process in Church and Synagogue* (New York: Guilford, 1991), 35.

6. Peter and Geri Scazzero, *Emotionally Healthy Relationships: Discipleship That Deeply Changes Your Relationship with Others (Workbook)* (Grand Rapids, Mich.: Zondervan, 2017), 131–32.

CHAPTER 8: THE GIFT OF FORGIVENESS

1. Bobby Allyn, "Ex-Dallas Officer Who Killed Man in His Own Apartment Is Found Guilty of Murder," NPR, October 1, 2019, www.npr. org/2019/10/01/765788338/ex-dallas-officer-who-killed-neighbor-in-upstairs-apartment-found-guilty-of-murd.

2. Giovanna Albanese, "Dead Victim's Brother Speaks of Christ, Extends Forgiveness to Convicted Officer," *Decision*, October 3, 2019, https:// decisionmagazine.com/dead-victims-brother-speaks-christ-extends-forgiveness -convicted-officer.

3. Miroslav Volf, *Free of Charge: Giving and Forgiving in a Culture Stripped of Grace* (Grand Rapids, Mich.: Zondervan, 2005), 15–16.

4. Volf, *Free of Charge*, 130.

5. See Frederick Dale Bruner's commentary on the gospel of Matthew for cultural background on this idea: *Matthew: A Commentary* (Grand Rapids, Mich.: Eerdmans, 2004), 561.

6. Dennis Linn, Sheila Fabricant Linn, and Matthew Linn, *Don't Forgive Too Soon: Extending the Two Hands That Heal* (New York: Paulist, 1997), iv, 29.

7. Molly Howes, *A Good Apology: Four Steps to Make Things Right* (New York: Grand Central, 2020).

8. William H. Willimon, *Thank God It's Friday: Encountering the Seven Last Words from the Cross* (Nashville: Abingdon, 2006), 11.

9. Henri Nouwen, paraphrased in Brennan Manning, *The Signature of Jesus: The Call to a Life Marked by Holy Passion and Relentless Faith* (Colorado Springs, Colo.: Multnomah, 2004), 149.

CHAPTER 9: LOVE IN PUBLIC

1. Howard Thurman, *Jesus and the Disinherited* (Boston: Beacon, 2012), 7.

2. Scot McKnight, *A Community Called Atonement*, Living Theology, ed. Tony Jones (Nashville: Abingdon, 2007), 124.

3. Fleming Rutledge, *The Crucifixion: Understanding the Death of Jesus Christ* (Grand Rapids, Mich.: Eerdmans, 2015), 134.

4. McKnight, *Community Called Atonement*, 236.

5. Tyler Conway, "James Blake, Former Tennis Star, Detained by Police in Case of Mistaken Identity," Bleacher Report, https://bleacherreport.com/ articles/2563853-james-blake-former-tennis-star-detained-by-police-in-case-of -mistaken-identity.

6. Abby Goodnough, "Harvard Professor Jailed; Officer Is Accused of Bias," *The New York Times,* July 20, 2009, https://nytimes.com/2009/07/21/us/21gates .html.

7. James H. Cone, *A Black Theology of Liberation* (Maryknoll, N.Y.: Orbis Books, 2010), 33.

8. Annie Correal and Desiree Rios, " 'It's Not Enough': Living Through a Pandemic on $100 a Week," *The New York Times,* May 23, 2021, https:// nytimes.com/interactive/2021/05/23/nyregion/undocumented-immigrants -poverty-nyc.html.

9. Ralph Ellison, *Invisible Man,* 2nd ed. (New York: Modern Library, 1994), 3.

10. Fyodor Dostoyevsky, *The Brothers Karamazov,* trans. Constance Garnett, Dover Thrift ed. (New York: Dover, 1998), 101.

11. I had trouble locating the exact source of this quote, but I'm certain I heard it from Hauerwas in one of his talks. He gets at something similar in the introduction of his book *Community of Character: Toward a Constructive Christian Social Ethic* (Notre Dame, Ind.: University of Notre Dame, 1991).

AFTERWORD

1. Ruth Burrows, *Living in Mystery* (New York: Sheed and Ward, 1999), 96.

2. Brennan Manning, *The Ragamuffin Gospel: Good News for the Bedraggled, Beat-Up, and Burnt Out* (Colorado Springs, Colo.: Multnomah, 2005), 25.

ABOUT THE AUTHOR

RICH VILLODAS is the author of *The Deeply Formed Life* (winner of the *Christianity Today* Book Award), and the Brooklyn-born lead pastor of New Life Fellowship, a large multiracial church with more than seventy-five countries represented, in Elmhurst, Queens. Rich graduated with a bachelor of arts in pastoral ministry and theology from Nyack College. He went on to complete his master of divinity from Alliance Theological Seminary. He enjoys reading widely and preaching and writing on contemplative spirituality, justice-related issues, and the art of preaching. He's been married to Rosie since 2006, and they have two beautiful children, Karis and Nathan.